THE RULE OF TASTE
From George I to George IV

John Steegman's entertaining study traces the various changes in the arts of gardening, architecture and painting from the early eighteenth century to the early nineteenth century.

Reprinted for the first time since 1936, Steegman gives an unprecedented insight into the minutae of classical living during the Georgian era, and is a valuable historical document as well as being of current interest. *The Rule of Taste* will enchant and delight the reader with its sensitivity and meticulous eye for detail.

The cover shows a watercolour of the Star Chamber, Carlton House, London

THE RULE OF TASTE
From George I to George IV

John Steegman

Century Hutchinson Ltd / The National Trust of Great Britain
London Melbourne Auckland Johannesburg

First published in 1936 by Macmillan & Co Ltd

© John Steegman 1936

All rights reserved

This edition first published in 1986 by Century Hutchinson Ltd
in association with the National Trust,
Brookmount House, 62–65 Chandos Place, London, WC2N 4NW

Century Hutchinson Publishing Group (Australia) Pty Ltd
PO Box 496, 16–22 Church Street, Hawthorn, Melbourne, Victoria
3122

Century Hutchinson Group (NZ) Ltd
PO Box 40–086, 32–34 View Road, Glenfield, Auckland 10

Century Hutchinson Group (SA) Pty Ltd
PO Box 337, Berglvei 2012, South Africa

ISBN 0 7126 9463 3

Published in association with the National Trust, this new
series is devoted to reprinting books on artistic, architectural,
social and cultural heritage of Britain. The imprint will cover
buildings and monuments, arts and crafts, gardening and
landscape in a variety of literary forms, including histories,
memoirs, biographies and letters.

The Century Classics also includes the Travellers, Seafarers
and Lives and Letters series.

Printed in Great Britain by
Richard Clay (The Chaucer Press) Ltd, Bungay, Suffolk

ITS dangerous tendency, added to its frequency, must plead my excuse for taking notice of the following vulgar mode of expression: 'I do not profess to understand these matters but I know what pleases me'.

HUMPHREY REPTON

CONTENTS

PAGE

INTRODUCTION ix

CHAPTER I

THE AUGUSTAN RULES 1

CHAPTER II

BAROQUE TO BURLINGTON 18

CHAPTER III

CHINESE AND ROCOCO 36

CHAPTER IV

SUBLIME AND PICTURESQUE 52

CHAPTER V

STRAWBERRY HILL AND FONTHILL 72

CHAPTER VI

COLLECTORS AND CRITICS 93

CHAPTER VII

THE AGE OF ADAM 114

vii

The Rule of Taste

CHAPTER VIII

INTRODUCTION

IN the following pages an attempt is made to trace the various changes in the arts of architecture, gardening and painting as reflected in the outlook of those classes of society which, from the early eighteenth to the early nineteenth centuries, recognised themselves as the payers of the piper and consequently the callers of the tune. The word "Taste" is used throughout because, though in many ways unsatisfactory, it remains perhaps the only single word which expresses both an immutable quality of discernment, criticism and perception, independent of special knowledge or training and independent of extraneous factors, and also an always active sensitiveness to temporary fashions; it can, thanks to the elasticity of our language, imply both standards and enthusiasms and can include both those who not only know what they like but know why they like it, and those who only know what the majority of other people like; it is used because, in fact, taste is both a quality which we find in certain gifted individuals and also a collective noun meaning merely tastes. Further, the title of this essay has been so chosen because the word "Rule" can also be applied in two ways; it may mean the exercise of sovereignty and direct authority or it may mean, again collectively, rules; thus "The Rule of Taste" is intended to imply both a régime in which Taste is paramount and a canon, or set of regulations, by which fashions in tastes are governed.

The existence of individuals endowed with the

power of discernment is not peculiar to the eighteenth or any other century, nor indeed is the tendency to assume that power on insufficient grounds; what is peculiar to the period is an apparently general agreement upon what constituted Correct taste, and an attempt to substitute the certainty of the Correct for the more doubtful True (or Good); while the definition of the latter must always be subjective and speculative, it is not impossible, given certain conditions, to define the former in a manner that at the moment seems final; given those conditions, the methods of defining are first the establishment of rules, then the establishment of rulers, and finally the establishment of a tradition of obedience to those rulers. Assuming that these methods are successful, the result will be that men's houses are built, their pictures and furniture chosen and their gardens and parks laid out in a manner which secures general approval, which is seldom criticised adversely and which establishes their owners as men of taste.

This essay is not concerned to examine the desirability of such a system in general, but its suitability to the conditions existing in Hanoverian England; its principal objects are to examine the reasons for the experiment being made; the measure of success it enjoyed during two-thirds of the eighteenth century; the gradual failure and abandonment of the experiment during the first third of the nineteenth century; and the political and social conditions which the need of such an experiment presupposes. But while the period discussed is roughly that from the government of Walpole in the 1730's to the passing of the Reform Bill in 1832, it may be considered desirable to review briefly the condition of the arts in the period immediately preceding.

Introduction

The history of the Fine Arts in England is not a subject that has attracted many scholars outside of England, but in this country and during the last few years there has been a perceptible awakening of interest in the English achievement and a growing consciousness of the facts that that achievement is not limited by the great names of Wren and Adam, of Hogarth, Reynolds and Gainsborough, and that outstanding artists such as these are distinguished from their contemporaries only by their superior gifts of expression and not by any essential difference in what they desired to express; that each is representative of his day and of his environment, and not an isolated phenomenon emerging from the traditional Anglo-Saxon fog. The achievement itself is there for us to judge, in museums, in churches and, above all, in private houses, but it must be judged fairly, not simply in relation to other and admittedly greater achievements, such as those of Italy or France, but in relation to the special conditions in which it was produced. Its historian must consider the effects of the overthrow of the monastic system and the old Church;[1] of the redistribution of wealth and the rise of new men, of the building of new houses on a new scale of splendour in a country still apart from Europe, and of the curiosity about that Europe which impelled men, from early in the seventeenth century, to travel either on the Grand Tour or to universities like Padua and Paris. This curiosity which engendered the habit of foreign travel engendered also the habit of collecting, for once it had become necessary for a young man to have travelled it became necessary for him to show some tangible results of his journeys; at first that was limited

[1] See Coulton, *Art and the Reformation*.

xi

to the French or Italian cut of his clothes and to his partiality for French or Italian poetry, but soon, and especially under the very highly cultivated Charles I, it became important for him to possess works of art and to spend large sums of money in acquiring a collection of antiquities, curiosities, medals, gems, statuary or paintings; the habit of collecting spread, encouraged by the examples of the Earl of Arundel, the Duke of Buckingham, the Earl of Pembroke, Sir Anthony Vandyck and the King himself; it gained impetus whenever a great collection, such as those of Rubens or the Duke of Mantua, was dispersed, but it was violently checked by the Civil War and the death or temporary eclipse of those who had most encouraged it; and after 1660 their successors, or themselves restored in fortune, were in a very different mind.

A comprehensive survey of the conditions governing the arts in England would probably show that the most important formative period in the development of our consciousness is the second half of the seventeenth century; between 1550 and 1650 men's minds had been occupied by the practical aspects of religion and politics more deeply than by any other forms of thought; philosophy was concerned more with the causes of phenomena than with their nature, and scientific knowledge was still to a large extent what the Middle Ages had remembered of classical learning; Hobbes had no following, standing then, as ever since, alone; Bacon had to await a posthumous fulfilment in Newton, and not even Harvey nor Browne could wholly escape what we now, not always rightly, dismiss as superstition. But the temper of the later seventeenth century was entirely different from that of the first half; the new

Introduction

passion for natural philosophy called the Royal Society
into being, and while certain great names stand out
above the others, they are typical rather than exceptional: Newton, Wren, Boyle, Evelyn represent the
spirit of their age, while Bacon and Harvey were at
variance with theirs. By 1700 standards had been set in
music, poetry, drama, painting and architecture which
were in close agreement with what was being most
admired in the more civilised capitals on the Continent,
and critical minds which had hitherto found their
highest satisfaction abroad could now be satisfied at
home. Shaftesbury[1] gave a lead to those, consciously
discerning, who wished to explore the principles on
which their discernment was based; and critical discrimination, or taste, became a fashion and almost a
habit with the small but important class of society at the
top. The effect of Shaftesbury's systematised philosophy
of aesthetic was seen mainly in a change of approach to
the visual arts, in an establishment of principles where
previously there had been little, if any, conscious reasoning and finally the hardening of those principles into a
set of rules for the critics' guidance. A similar process
had already begun much earlier in English poetry, for
Edmund Waller on the eve of the Civil War was trying
to introduce a new and more rigid system of prosody
in place of the metrical looseness which he regarded as
a grave danger; in place of the romantically expressed
feeling and rather shapeless fancy, which threatened
at any moment to sink into the turgid, he brought precision of statement expressed in highly organised couplets
and for extravagance he substituted discipline. Waller
was not, in truth, wholly successful in his mission and,

[1] 3rd Earl of Shaftesbury, *Letter concerning Design*, 1709.

as Bacon had to await the advent of Newton, he had to await the advent of Dryden for his fulfilment; the complete supremacy of Pope which followed in the next generation inaugurated a rule of severe training by which the main body of English poetry was governed till the close of the eighteenth century and by which it was able to survive the difficult birth of such poets as Keats or Coleridge without being subsequently enfeebled. The victory of Pope, and through him of Dryden and Waller, may be dated from the appearance of *The Dunciad* in 1712; three years earlier Shaftesbury had published his *Letter concerning Design*, and three years later the Georgian age was successfully inaugurated with the collapse of the Jacobite Rising.

The moment was auspicious: by a combination of political and economic causes Britain had once again come into the front rank of European states, for the Whig Revolution and the Marlborough wars had re-established her greatness and given her authority, stability, self-confidence and wealth which during the coming ministry of Sir Robert Walpole were to be confirmed into a tradition. The governing class was small and closely preserved against intrusion from below, an oligarchy concentrating wealth and power together within its own circle and, though very conscious of the advantages to itself, conscious also of the responsibility such a system implied; they saw themselves as a class, independent both of the multitude and of the Crown, who by reason of their birth, possessions, traditions and education were alone fitted to rule and in whose hands lay the remaking of England through the training and control of public opinion, without consulting or even pretending to consult the ordinary citizen. This consciousness of the responsibilities and duties of their position was extended until it completely filled their minds and governed all their activities, and to their guidance is due eighteenth-century England, her achievements in arts and letters, in politics, war and conquest, her laws and her Constitution; when the time came and the fashion of a romantic democracy began to invade even England, then the control was relaxed and handed over, not willingly and not completely, into the hands of a new controlling class with the new traditions of industrial and commercial wealth. The following chapters are in the nature of a review of the relations existing between the men who paid and the artists working for them, of the part played in the English artistic achievement by the Man of Taste and of that achievement itself, with the factors which successively influenced it, during the establishment, progress and decline of a system which was never absolute but was certainly severe; a system which had its origin in an intellectual *défaitisme*[1] and a material pride and self-confidence, and in the concentration of wealth and both political and social authority in the hands of one small, unchallenged class, sophisticated, civilised and, except for purposes of sport, urban in its inclinations.

The customary text-books suggest that English history has been made by the priests and statesmen, the sailors and soldiers and the industrialists and merchants, a view which is neither wholly true nor wholly untrue. It is not untrue in that these are the men responsible for the economic and constitutional foundation on which the structure of England is based, but it is untrue in suggesting that their work is the whole fabric

---

[1] See *infra*, Chapter II.

of that structure. England as we know her to-day, in relation to the rest of Europe, is a product of the eighteenth and nineteenth centuries, for the seventeenth century marks in its first half a retrogression from the point reached under the Tudors and, in its second half, a determination to set about recovery. Revolution and change of dynasty accomplished the recovery in its more spectacular aspects, but in the world of mind as opposed to action recovery was no less desirable and the methods employed no less revolutionary; Walpole, Chatham and Pitt, who formed the political character of England, are not more important than Pope or Johnson, Wesley or Wilberforce or Hogarth, Gainsborough, Fielding or Robert Adam. In the particular aspect of the eighteenth century here discussed the most prominent names are not those of statesmen, but of men who in relation to that particular aspect wielded a statesmanlike authority. Wren, Burlington, Kent, Hogarth, Chambers, Reynolds, Burke, Payne Knight, Humphrey Repton, John Nash, with Frederick Prince of Wales and George IV, are seen as the upholders of a system of control whose disappearance with the advent of an industrial and more democratic society had on the arts an effect comparable to that which a disappearance of statesmanship might have (or has had) on the political well-being of England.

CHAPTER I

THE AUGUSTAN RULES

THERE is a corner by the Orangery at Hampton Court where the bricks of two great ages meet, and the manner of their meeting symbolises a victory without a conflict. Wolsey had built himself a palace and King William III, succeeding in due course to its possession, caused Wren to magnify it. A modern architect, swayed perhaps unwillingly by the associations of history and hampered by a respect for the past, might have compromised in an attempt to make the new fit the old; but Wren, who was certainly not lacking in respect for the past, made tradition his servant, not his master; with the confidence of genius in his own supremacy he needed not to make concessions to something smaller and less important, for the proximity of Gothic windows and twisted chimney-stacks and busy Tudor detail could not seriously endanger the splendour of his own conception, which does, in fact, gain much in dignity by the contrast. He did not attempt to make the new fit the old; they met in one corner, and Wren's triumph over Wolsey was established.

That is typical of the attitude adopted at the end of the seventeenth century towards what must, for lack of a more precise word, be called comprehensively Gothic. To thoughtful observers of that age Gothic appeared to be disordered, to lack cohesion; there was no rhythm, no rule, above all there was no scholarship about it; not only was it restless, it was untidy. The new century was to show a new spirit, the spirit of order; the reason, not the heart, was to govern man in all his works, for there had been enough exuberance and excitement; it was time to check that now, to retard if possible the rate of production in order to heighten the standard of achievement. Man felt that he was beginning to grow out of his Renaissance youth, and that it was time for him to begin collecting and arranging the experiences of his adolescence, and from them to formulate rules that might enable him to live in future as a qualified Citizen of the World.

The England of the people was still very much the same as it had been under James I or Charles I, and was to continue unchanged in essence until the industrial, commercial and agricultural revolution under George III. But the England of the educated and governing classes was changing, chiefly by reason of the closer contact with French thought and the experience of French manners; the Paris of Louis XIV, as reflected in letters and architecture, was ordered and civilised to an extent which made London seem, to those who had experienced the other, somewhat provincial and out of date. At first only a few were sensitive to this reproach or were even aware that there was anything with which they might be reproached; the majority were complacent in the restoration of the traditional order, honouring the King, fearing God and hating the Pope and the French; indulgent towards Nell Gwyn as the "Protestant whore", resentful of Louise de Kéroualle as the Papist; forgetful of Cromwell's triumphs in diplomacy and war abroad, they were content to be citizens of a little State with a glorious Elizabethan past, and only after the Revolution of 1688 did ambition begin to awake in the mass of the people. Among the thoughtful and the active ambition and the desire for improvement had been awake for more than a decade, and their influence was certainly, though slowly, effective in an ever-increasing degree and was helped by the Revolution.

The Revolution of 1688 brought about a change more than merely political; it gave England a confidence in her own strength, a self-reliance which had been lost for nearly a century; she went to war with France, and was not beaten; she went to war with France again, and Blenheim sent up her opinion of herself to a point it had not reached since the days of the Armada. England was once more a great power abroad, with a stable government at home; the collapse of the Stuart pretensions in 1715 gave the House of Hanover a better introduction to the English people than that dynasty could ever have managed for itself. And the accession to power of Robert Walpole inaugurated a period of peace that lasted twenty years, that enabled England, having established herself in the eyes of Europe and made herself more nearly the equal of her neighbours, to embark on that slow process of civilisation which, aided by the necessary increase of wealth, was to bring her at last into the front rank.

The reign of George I cannot be included among the more stirring epochs of our history; politically it was a sordid, corrupt and successful period of stagnation; socially it lacked the brilliance of the Restoration or the elegance of the 1760's. It stands to us as an age without imagination, without character; that is because we tend to see it in relation to other and more definite ages, those of Elizabeth, for example, or Charles II or the

3

Prince Regent. Examined by itself, it will be seen to be, so to speak, trying to make a fresh start. The only way to avoid the mistakes and stupidities of adolescence was, it was felt, to make rigid rules for its own guidance and never to depart from the canon thus established. To those who valued the things of the mind England undoubtedly seemed awkward, *gauche* and uncivilised, irrational and graceless; in short, she was seen to be in need of education and polish. It was time to stop being young and romantic; the dying fires of the Renaissance had no longer any warmth, so the ashes must be raked up and new fires be lighted, built in a sounder and more scientific manner.

Thus the Augustan age began, the age of rule, of reason and of order; when man began at last to assert his authority over Nature, when the Muses became, collectively, his servant rather than his mistress and even the Gods themselves were kept strictly in the place appointed them. Renaissance painters had been fond of painting such subjects as "The Muse inspiring a Poet", with the poet waiting hopefully and patiently on his mistress's caprice; but the Augustan poet never waited thus, never had need to wait; he called for his Muse and she came. He began to learn her language, and found it surprisingly easy, so easy that he was tempted to summon her on every possible occasion. And she, poor hard-working creature, heroically responded, but she realised, though kept the knowledge to herself, that the standard of service demanded of her was not, perhaps, very high; her masters were easily satisfied, and so long as she behaved herself, came when called and observed the rules and regulations laid down for her conduct, everybody would be well pleased.

The Augustan Rules

As a result of this new spirit of rule, a change was visible in society. Persons of Quality were no longer always content to be only that; they felt that they had too long ignored other things and they must now become Persons of Taste; it was part of the desire to catch up, to repair past omissions, part of the new self-consciousness. Taste had been lacking, therefore taste must be acquired, but before it could be acquired it must be defined, and its application in any given direction having been defined it must be formalised. Formularised too, if necessary; "formula" has about it a suggestion of the diminutive, and it has always, indeed, been a refuge for smaller minds; but while the lesser Augustans evolved and clung to their formulae, even the greatest were in their essence formal; Pope and Kneller are always intensely formal. But since an easy formula was ever ready at hand, there was a constant temptation (since the most active brain has its moments of inactivity) to employ it. That is why men of this period of whom one demands the most are so often disappointing; perhaps Pope alone never disappoints; his skill was greater, his brain more active, than those of his contemporaries, though Addison certainly wrote prose almost as faultless as Pope's verse; Swift might have had, had he kept it unimpaired, a vision as keen and penetrating, but he allowed it to be distorted by the poison that corrupted his whole mind. While the "little monster of Twit'nam" may have become occasionally shrill through excessive ill-temper, even in his most peevish moments he kept his sense of proportion, but Swift, on the other hand, with all his fierce wit, shows throughout his life that lack of balance and symmetry that became in his last years insanity. Form and proportion, once the principles were grasped and thoroughly understood, took precedence over all other qualities. To the classically ordered mind Shakespeare must always be a little shocking, and the Augustans were certainly shocked, as the French were, by his want of art, his barbarous ignoring of the rules; but those, already only a few, to whom rules were still a means rather than the end itself refused to deprive themselves altogether of Lear or Hamlet;[1] even to them, these were spiritually important, and the difficulty could easily be solved by encasing them in new garments cut more in accordance with the dictates of Good Taste; from Dryden to Garrick, Shakespeare was so ordered. His often-proclaimed immortality is by nothing more clearly proved than by this, that he survived the Augustan age. Nothing else can kill him.

The danger of making rules is not that they are difficult to observe, but that they are easy to observe too rigidly; they should guide, not dictate. For the first half, indeed for the greater part, of the eighteenth century the minds and spirits of men were dominated by rules. They were formulated in the first instance when their absence was suddenly realised, when a guide was desperately needed, and as time went on they became, like old servants, masterful. This is particularly true in the arts of painting and architecture, and is one of the reasons why under Queen Anne and the first two Georges architecture was so fine and painting so poor. Bad architecture is primarily the result of ignorance, while bad painting means lack of individuality; an architect with learning and knowledge, even if he lack

[1] Dryden said, writing of Corneille, "I admire the pattern of elaborate writing—but I love Shakespeare".

6

personality, can still build a tolerably good house, but no amount of training can make a painter produce even a tolerably good picture if he were not capable of painting one without that instruction. There were as few good painters in the early Georgian as there have been in any other age, but even the few there were generally found themselves crushed by the regulations. Kneller would probably have been a better painter at any other moment in our history; that is not to say that he would have done even better than he actually did at his best, but that he might well have achieved that best more often if he had not had to observe so closely the rules of correct taste; he was not an imaginative man, but he shows upon occasion that in a freer atmosphere his brain would have worked more quickly. In certain of his portraits he makes it clear that had he reached maturity under Charles II he would have been a formidable rival to Lely. The difference between the two is emphasised at Hampton Court in the two series of Court beauties' portraits; Lely is concerned to make a distinct and individual picture in each case, and succeeds in doing so, while Kneller is concerned to paint a large number of Court ladies in the manner prescribed for portraits of Court ladies; whether or not the sitters were beautiful is to us irrelevant, for they were considered so by the critics of their own day; William's Court being Dutch, George I's being German and Sir Godfrey himself being German, the qualifications for a "Beauty" were perhaps less exacting than at the more critical Court of Charles II. The comparative goodness or badness of taste is, after all, less important, since such standards change every few years, than the rigidity or otherwise of the canons which at any one moment define that taste; the canons of taste in Kneller's day were already being fixed and were rapidly to become rigid, so rigid, indeed, that no painter could dispense with them, whether he were English or foreign; Kneller, Dahl, Van Loo, Wissing, Jervas, Thornhill, even Jonathan Richardson, all were successful so long as they were correct, and took care, therefore, to be correct always.

Hogarth alone revolted, and alone he was never accepted; he wanted Taste, as Shakespeare wanted Art; but while Shakespeare could be trimmed and altered, Hogarth must be taken or rejected whole. It was not that his contemporaries resented his satire, for Pope had been almost rapturously acclaimed, but that he opposed everything which they had been with such care establishing; neither his portraits nor his conversation-pieces were accused of being in bad taste, they were accused of not being in the correct taste; a very different thing, for if a work was not in the correct manner it was waste of time to consider whether it was good or bad. But even Hogarth, though he may have been a rebel in practice, conformed in theory; or at least in one theory, that of Ideal Beauty.

The defining of Taste by rule is equivalent to saying what is and what is not beautiful; the eighteenth century was wise in providing itself so complacently with an answer to what we ourselves find unanswerable. We have a standard inch, a standard foot, and a standard yard, and standard pennyweights, pecks and perches, but we have not got a standard beautiful face; moreover, we have temporarily given up trying to find it. As a matter of fact, the eighteenth century had not found it either, but it never gave up the search and always maintained that it existed. If nobody actually formulated Ideal Beauty, everybody was agreed at least as to the general lines to which it must conform, just as everybody in general was agreed as to who had been the greatest poets, painters or sculptors. The approved procedure was to observe the types most frequently portrayed by each of the masters, by Raphael and Carlo Dolci, by Michelangelo and the sculptors of the Laocoon and the Medici Venus, to measure them and combine them, and then in theory to produce the Ideal. Hogarth's *Analysis of Beauty* was "written with a view to fixing the fluctuating Ideas of Taste";[1] he searched for what he thought to be the basic fact of Beauty; he found it, not in an abstract quality such as Grace, or the Sublime, but in a geometrical formula, an S-shaped curve, and upon this spiral rested everything that was beautiful, in nature or in art.

The publication of Hogarth's *Analysis* is such an important event in the history of Taste that it is worth listening a little to what he says. He only arrives at his mathematical conclusion after carefully considering what others have demanded in their search for beauty; he quotes Pythagoras in support of Variety, and also Shakespeare (". . . nor custom stale her infinite variety"); he instances the "Hercules by Glicon" as an example of Fitness, and proves that if he had lived 200 years later he would have acclaimed the beauty of machinery; he praises Variety and Uniformity, Simplicity and Intricacy; he quotes Du Fresnoy and De Piles on their *Je ne sais quoi* and calls it Grace; Windsor Castle and the robes of judges illustrate the Sublime, which he calls Quantity, and holds to be of high im-

---

[1] See title-page to 1st edition, 1753.

portance: "Elephants and whales please us with their unwieldy greatness. Even large personages, merely for being so, command respect"; and again: "the full-bottomed wig, like the lion's mane, hath something noble in it and adds not only dignity but sagacity to the countenance". On the subject of Elegance, another indispensable quality, Hogarth says some remarkable things, amongst them being the theory that we do not laugh at what is elegant, and do laugh at what is not. "What can it be", he says, "that makes a whole audience burst into laughter when they see the miller's sack, in Dr. Faustus, jumping cross the stage? Was a well-shaped vase to do the same it would equally surprise, but not make everybody laugh, because the elegance of the form would prevent it." He feels clearly that beauty in whatever manifestation is primarily a matter of line; starting from that premise, he must find a line that combines all the qualities of Elegance, Grace, Simplicity, Variety, Distinctness and so on; obviously such a line cannot be straight for such "vary only in length and therefore are least ornamental"; after much examination the ideal line, the Line of Beauty, is established as a spiral curving not only in linear direction, but in its planes also. It may not be irrelevant to quote Sir Joshua Reynolds, who said[1] to a correspondent thirty years later, "Your idea of producing the line of beauty by taking the medium of the two extremes, exactly co-incides with my idea, and its beauty I think may fairly be deduced from habit. All lines are either curved or straight, and that which partakes equally of each is the medium or average of all lines and therefore more

[1] Letter to James Beattie, 31st March 1782. See *Letters of Sir Joshua Reynolds,* ed. Frederick Whiley Hilles, 1929.

beautiful than any other line; notwithstanding this, an artist would act preposterously that should take every opportunity to introduce this line into his works, as Hogarth himself did, who appears to have taken an aversion to a straight line. His pictures, therefore, want that line of firmness and stability which is produced by straight lines; this conduct may truly be said to be unnatural, for it is not the conduct of nature."

Hogarth decided that such a line was at once the foundation and the epitome of beauty, and, finding that line very often to be seen in the Antique, maintained consequently that the Antique was superior to the Modern. His older contemporary, Jonathan Richardson,[1] believing that the qualities of Grace and Greatness were the essential components of Beauty, and finding these to exist in the Antique, formed the same idea of the superiority of antiquity, mentioning at the same time certain modern (as opposed to ancient) painters who possessed one or the other of these qualities; as, for examples, Correggio, who had "Grace not inferior to Parmegiano and rather more Greatness"; Annibale Carracci, who "was rather great than genteel, though he was that too"; "Rubens," continues Richardson, "was great, but raised upon a Flemish idea"; "Salvator's landscapes are great; the style of the Borgognone is great". He admired Leonardo for his Grace and a promise of Greatness, but he more admired Michelangelo, who, in addition to Greatness in the utmost degree, also possessed "a fine seasoning of Grace"; his praise of Titian, Tintoretto and Veronese is qualified by saying that "they

---

[1] Jonathan Richardson: *Essay on the Theory of Painting*, 1715; *Essay on the Art of Criticism in Relation to Painting*, 1719; *Argument in Behalf of the Science of a Connoisseur*, 1719.

have Grace and Greatness, but it is not antique"; finally, Vandyck "had something of both these good qualities, but not much nor always". In his essay on the *Science of a Connoisseur* Richardson returns again to the Antique as the criterion; he says, "The Painters of the Roman school were the best designers and had more of the antique taste in their works than any of the others . . . those of Florence were good designers, and had a kind of Greatness, but it was not antique. The Venetian and Lombard schools had . . . a certain Grace, but entirely modern and their knowledge of the Antique very little. . . . The works of those of the German school have a dryness and ungraceful stiffness . . . odious, and as remote from the Antique as Gothicism could carry it. The Flemings have been good colourists and imitated nature as they conceived it. . . . Rubens himself lived and died a Fleming, though he would fain have been an Italian. The French . . . as they have not the German stiffness nor the Flemish ungracefulness, neither have they the Italian solidity; and in their airs of heads and manners they are easily distinguished from the Antique, how much soever they may have endeavoured to imitate them." Since, therefore, the Antique seemed to be the highest expression of beauty, it was clear that Apelles must have been the greatest of painters; that point was never disputed, for the admirable reason that neither Richardson nor Hogarth nor anyone else had ever seen one single line drawn by him, nor any reproduction or copy of such a line, nor had or could have the smallest idea of his works; but his name had survived, they saw him referred to in terms of high praise, he was a contemporary of the great sculptors, and that was enough.

The Augustan Rules

Hogarth's *Analysis of Beauty* is confined to the definition of what is ideally beautiful. Richardson begins at an earlier point and goes further; his *Theory of Painting* is almost entirely technical, and deals with such matters as Invention, Expression, Composition, Design, Colouring and Handling; the *Art of Criticism* discusses what is meant by the "Goodness of a Picture" and the proper laying-down of rules, as well as technical points such as the knowledge of hands and means of recognising the different masters; while the *Science of a Connoisseur* emphasises the social importance of a Gentleman of Taste and the civilising influence of art upon a nation, by "the reformation of our manners, refinement of our pleasures and increase of our fortunes and reputation". So far he has said nothing that might not equally have been said at any time after 1660, but here the early eighteenth century speaks in its own particular voice— "the business of painting is not only to represent nature and to make the best choice of it, but to raise and improve it". Richardson would never have laid it down that the business of art is merely to hold up the mirror to Nature, or if he had none of his contemporaries would have agreed with him. Nature was the raw, very raw, material out of which the artist had to make something acceptable, what was acceptable being dictated not by the artist himself but by the general agreement of persons of taste; such agreement, moreover, being in that well-ordered age not only possible but actually achieved.

Nature was only admired when she resembled art, when, in fact, she became "picturesque". Picturesque is a word with which we are to-day only too familiar; we know that it is often used as a synonym for "quaint", which was once a very good word, or for "pretty", which also was once a very good word; it frequently implies decay, it being well known that a cottage or barn on the verge of falling down makes a far stronger appeal than one that is thoroughly sound; peasants are picturesque, and Elizabethan cottages and barges and old women in sun-bonnets and cows standing in the shade of elms; "what a picture they would make!" we cry, implying thereby that we think them picturesque. But this unhappy word has had its meaning completely reversed, for when it was first applied to any scene, it meant, not that an artist ought to paint it, but that it looked as if it already had been painted, that it resembled a picture; the more a scene resembled a picture, the more beautiful it was, and, moreover, the number of kinds of picture that it was desirable for Nature to resemble was limited. For three-quarters of the eighteenth century Nature did not seem tender or gentle; she was neither intimate nor sympathetic, she was not romantic and she was not tragic; in short, she was hardly ever considered except in her relation to man; she was uncouth, ignorant, unpolished and unreliable, and if she was to be allowed into gentlemen's houses she must first be taken in hand and civilised; and the man whose business it was to do that was the artist. Landscape for its own sake was not in great demand, but certain painters like Canaletto, Samuel Scott, Brooking, Wootton and the Smiths of Chichester had something of a vogue, though it is doubtful if any of them, except Canaletto, was considered quite sufficiently correct; Richard Wilson was perhaps the only landscape painter in England who was considered the equal of the great Italian masters like Claude and the Poussins. Wilson's great contemporary reputation was founded on his classic landscapes, organised and built up with a scholarship worthy of a Roman (which, as a young man, he practically was); but that reputation was wrecked by his later "English" pictures, for in them he seemed altogether to have forgotten the precepts of Claude; useless for him to point out that the cool silver and green of England was not the blazing blue and gold of Italy, that the Thames and the Wye and the Tiber were not all the same river; the answer admitted of no argument, Claude and Nicolas Poussin were French just as he was English, but they had got over that disability and he must too; he had shown that he could paint as well as they in the high Roman style, and he must continue to do so. He did not, and his life closed in poverty and disappointment.

Landscape, generally, was not in great demand for it was felt that the aim of a painter should be higher; he should not be content merely with improving Nature, but he should endeavour to "communicate ideas, whereby mankind is advanced higher in the rational state and made better", as Richardson says. He must communicate ideas of a lofty, noble and tragic character by painting scenes from history or poetry that illustrate those qualities, such as the incident of Count Ugolino, for example. Even Hogarth tried, once, to paint in the grand, Italian and elevated manner, but his "Sigismunda" has not generally been considered a success. To quote Jonathan Richardson yet once more: "I believe there never was such a race of men upon the face of the earth, never did men look and act like those we see represented in the works of Raphael, Michelangelo, Correggio and Parmegiano . . . we rarely or never see such landscapes as those of Titian, Carracci, Salvator Rosa, Claude Lorrain, Jasper Poussin and Rubens. Such buildings and magnificence as in the pictures of Paolo Veronese. Our ideas . . . are raised and improved in the hands of a good painter, and the mind is thereby filled with the noblest, and therefore the most delightful, images." Portrait-painting, too, had to be elevated in the same manner; mere face-painting was not enough, the painter must bring out and emphasise the "beauty, good-sense, breeding and other good qualities of the person"; if, moreover, such qualities were absent all portrait-painters, at least from Vandyck to Lawrence, with the exception of Hogarth, considered it their duty to supply them. The low must be elevated, the irregular made straight, Nature improved on.

With all that Richardson says we should not perhaps agree to-day; a modern historical critic might not mention Parmigiano in the same breath as Leonardo da Vinci or name Jasper Poussin to the exclusion of Nicolas; we generally demand that a portrait-painter should tell us what a man is rather than what he ought to be or might be. We may safely assume that Richardson was not defining his own taste (for it is precisely the qualities that he mentions which his own portraits lack, and we value those portraits because they are such honest records of actual character), but the taste that those around and, especially, above him had formed. As the small upper section of society was rigidly controlling the distribution of wealth and power, in the belief that if they did not there would be no control, so they also controlled as rigidly the rules of Good Taste, believing that if they did not that too would vanish. During the remainder of the eighteenth century, taste underwent many changes, but the control, though at times less rigid than at others, remained always in the same hands; a tradition was formed and handed on, a little altered now and then in its progress; but in the main the dictates of the Augustans were obeyed, and the supremacy of the Ancients and the existence of the Ideal were alike hardly called into question.

CHAPTER II

BAROQUE TO BURLINGTON

THIS tradition, which bore as its fruit the very English arts of Georgian England, has really two separate roots; one of these is in the individualist temperament which has characterised the people of this island ever since the time when they first became conscious of their nationality and which is most pronounced under the Tudors; the other lies in a sense of inferiority, almost a *défaitisme*, not at all characteristic of the nation as a whole, but often seen among the intellectuals, especially in the later seventeenth century; a conviction that English civilisation must always be inferior to that of the Latin peoples. It was this belief, which certainly was confirmed by experience, that caused most thinking men after the Restoration to base their criticism on the achievements of France or Italy and, in balancing against those the achievements of their own country, to find the latter sadly lacking in anything of which they could be proud and to look to France as their only hope; but they ignored, or at least underestimated, the importance of their own inherited Englishness, and in trying to classicise, or latinise, their arts they perhaps did not realise that they could at the most but graft a foreign scion on to the native tree; the tree itself was too deep-rooted to be overthrown, and its Tudor growth was imperishable. Yet the observer of 1670, looking back over the preceding century, might be forgiven for

18

discounting his forebears' achievements in politics, since so little had been proved permanent, and from the crumbling of the Tudor fabric (or rather façade, for the invisible but solid foundations remained), not unnaturally he deduced a rottenness in the ornaments; in weighing the advantages of the new Continental policy against the old Nationalism, it was almost inevitable that he should wish to Continentalise the arts as well. And in this his instinct was probably right, for, except in lyric poetry and the inexplicable miracle of Shakespeare, the arts had produced nothing in this country comparable to the fruits of the Renaissance in France and Italy.

Yet under Elizabeth, England had become politically important and, relative to her size, powerful; the destruction of Spanish sea-power and decline of the Spanish menace in the Netherlands had given her both a new security and a greatly increased wealth, for although most of the treasure of the New World still went, and for a long time was to continue going, to Spain yet much of it found its way to England, and Sir Walter Raleigh was already pointing out to his fellow-countrymen the way to achieve a new and transpontine greatness. With the horizon thus widening, and brightening as it widened, it was natural that great men should have felt themselves at last great men; the Queen, who had succeeded to the rather precarious throne of a minor State, saw herself in the end one of the great Princes of Europe, a Monarch; to this high eminence her counsellors and advisers had helped her, and it had pleased her to reward their services in a suitably impressive, yet not too costly, manner; she bestowed land upon them and they, becoming thus the lords of many acres, set to work to build houses on a scale to equal their new splendour; Elizabeth prudently followed the example of her father in ennobling new men and surrounding herself with a grateful aristocracy that owed its elevation and much of its wealth to the bounty of her House. These new founders of great families were determined that their children and grandchildren should not lack hereditary splendour as they had done, and very soon in the vast and newly enclosed parks houses appeared larger, more luxurious and of more magnificent appearance than any that had yet been built in England. It was the age of Knole, of Hardwick, Hatfield and Ham, of Audley End and Haddon Hall.

These great Elizabethan and Jacobean mansions are the perfect expressions of the men who built them and lived in them; they imply enormous wealth and their small ill-lighted rooms, busily fretted ceilings, countless stairways and general lack of organisation, the elaborate ornamentation of the façades, the heavy, bulbous furniture, the mixture of great and little, all these suggest a generation in which there was still much of the medieval: the tables, cupboards and beds are fitted for a fortified castle rather than a house, so massive, ponderous and barbaric are they. A certain domestic quality is added by the great galleries which often run the whole length of one side, but it is seldom possible to regard a house of this period as a complete architectural whole; it has grown apparently at haphazard, the plan seems to have rambled over the ground. Nor was it even wholly English; strange foreign rules and principles were introduced, and if the house of the period was larger and more splendid than its predecessors, its splendour was often Italianate or Germanic.

Such houses were of the country of Spenser, "romanci-call" and medieval, while those that Inigo Jones was soon to build were of the country that Ben Jonson would have liked to create.

Inigo Jones paid two visits to Italy, and by the time that he had begun to make his name in England a re-volution in architecture was already being heralded. That revolution was brought about by the belated in-troduction of what must be the foundation of all great building, scholarship. We need not bewail the fact that Inigo Jones derived his learning from the study of Palladio, or maintain that his work is merely imitative; if he had been content to continue working in the tra-dition of those who built Hatfield or Holland House, he would still have been following in alien footsteps, for there was no purely English tradition that an architect could follow unless he were to spend his life build-ing either cathedrals or tithe-barns. At Whitehall and Greenwich Inigo Jones produced the first buildings of the Renaissance in England, the first buildings that can safely pass the most severe critical test and not have to depend on their associations or their "picturesqueness". Inigo Jones has never properly emerged from the shadow thrown over him by the Civil War; if that calamity had not occurred, Whitehall would have been com-pletely built as he designed it, and might be still ac-claimed as the greatest building in Northern Europe; it is not often that in England so great an artist has so understanding a patron as Charles I. It is, on the other hand, conceivable that but for another disaster an even greater artist might have remained relatively obscure; the Great Fire of 1666 gave Wren the opportunity of his life. Once the principles of Italian, or more narrowly,

Palladian architecture were mastered, the art in England entered on that glorious period that lasted till Adam brought it to an end. All the greater architects from Inigo Jones to Sir William Chambers used the rules of Palladio; they might adapt or modify them, as the variations of taste dictated, but the principles remained substantially the same. The earlier master is the classic of the school, while Wren, with less of pure scholarship and more of imagination, added something that can best be described as Baroque.

Baroque is nowadays a somewhat dangerous word to use, as it will probably conjure up visions of Würzburg, or the Fountain of Trevi, or the Abbey of Melk. Compared with the Karlskirche in Vienna, perhaps neither St. Paul's Cathedral nor St. Stephen's Walbrook are obviously baroque, but when they are compared with any work of Inigo Jones that appears the only adjective that will sufficiently emphasise the difference. What we generally mean by baroque needs, primarily, a hard, clear atmosphere with strong contrasts of light and shade and an accompanying splendour and extravagance that neither Dutch nor Hanoverian England could sufficiently supply; it also obviously flourishes more luxuriantly in a Catholic country, in fact it is almost incompatible with Protestantism. Wren, therefore, could never be baroque as Bernini or Fischer von Erlach were; yet the steeples he built for his fifty churches, his façades and his interiors possess that rich quality of movement and variety with which the successors of Palladio, the architects of the *seicento*, were bringing to life the more static dignity of the high Renaissance.

With such a rush during the last few years has the

baroque come into its own that half Europe has stood enraptured in Salzburg or made long excursions to see a fountain or a chapel, unstarred by Baedeker but underlined by Sitwell. "Baroque" and "rococo" are no longer confused as they used to be or used as synonyms, and so far have we moved from the Ruskinian habit of using those words contemptuously, of dismissing any tawdriness as baroque, that we would as soon describe all Gothic as "flamboyant". Ecclesiastical baroque was disapproved in the nineteenth century because it was felt to be unchristian; by some it was felt to be pagan, by others papist, but even papists themselves, like Pugin, felt it to be less Christian than the Gothic; this disapproval was intensified by failure to understand or sympathise with the motive behind the outward theatricality. The twisted columns in churches, the broken pediments, the billowing clouds and flying angels, the curving surfaces and serpentine lines, the cunningly concealed windows that throw dramatic sunbeams on to this or that saint, even the sometimes eccentric ground-plan itself, all were designed to carry the eye of the entering worshipper continuously towards the point above the High Altar where rested the Host, allowing it to light in its progress upwards on whatever devotional object the architect might select. But as Faith began to shrink and wither in the icy blasts of Reason, those who believed outwardly in the Church still demanded something to take the place of piety, for their appetites could not be satisfied by logic; therefore the priests were forced to call the theatre to their aid and borrowed from it the Dramatic, the Surprising and the Sensational. So the Catholic Church survived even the eighteenth century.

All baroque begins and ends in Rome; it may spread northwards to Austria and Bavaria, westwards to Spain, Portugal and Latin-America, but its complicated psychology and even more complicated physiology are for ever bound up with the psychology of a religion and the physiology of a city. This Roman connection would have been quite enough, by itself, to have prejudiced the chances of the baroque in post-1688 England; but in addition to the anti-Catholic feeling that characterised the average Englishman at the beginning of the eighteenth century, there was his individualism and insularity, his tendency to caution, his dislike of the exuberant, the excitable or anything that advanced too rapidly; it is perhaps hardly necessary to limit those qualities to the beginning of the eighteenth century. But for whatever reason, the Englishman was quite right in having nothing much to do with baroque; not that the entire *seicento* was ignored in this country; it was critically examined, a little of it borrowed and adapted, and the rest rejected. Putting aside the globe-like, balloon-like, cloud-like later accretions of the style, the prime innovation remains movement. The buildings of Wren, whether his churches or his country-houses, whether an Orangery or Hampton Court itself, show a scholarship that makes him there almost the equal of Inigo Jones, a scholarship, however, that was always his servant and never his master. There is about his work an easy, rich humanity, the same humanity as there is in Kneller's portrait of him in the National Portrait Gallery; the brain behind those eyes could rise with Newton's to the petrified beauty of pure mathematics, but the possessor of such hands was not going to be content with petrifaction. The vast genius of

Newton gleams arctically down upon us from some im-measurable distance. "God said, Let Newton be . . .": there can be no other explanation; we feel that he can crystallise any human experience into the few arid, final words of a physical law. But the genius of Wren works in the opposite direction, for stones, and the laws that govern their placing, are by him warmed, vitalised until to look at them is in itself an epitome of most human experience. Wren is in a sense comparable with Rubens; his great works have the same steady continuous movement as has the *Château de Steen*, a compound of experiment and experience.

Not that Wren was either the first architect to use the baroque in England, or the architect who used it most extensively. The York House Water-Gate near Charing Cross shows that Inigo Jones was experiment-ing in that direction before Wren was born; and when Wren was already getting old he saw elegant Sir John Vanbrugh piling up Blenheim and Castle Howard. At Greenwich his own work was decorated inside by Sir James Thornhill, who flung his gods and goddesses, his Muses, Graces, Vices, Virtues and King William and Queen Mary across the lofty ceiling of the Painted Hall, an English but no less courageous Verrio. Vanbrugh, at forty, took to architecture; he read the correct books, studied the rules and began; the results were like nothing that had been built in England before. Blenheim and Castle Howard possess several of the qualities that Hogarth was later to include in his Ideal: Variety, Quantity, Intricacy; they have been condemned and praised alternately ever since they were com-pleted, for the reason that they contain between them almost every reason there is both for and against the baroque. Vanbrugh was an artist first, an architect second; he was satisfied with Blenheim as a spectacle, for as such he had regarded it from the beginning; with its occupier's more domestic view of it, as a house, he could have but little sympathy. The friendship and support of Lord Carlisle was of the greatest service to Vanbrugh, for through him he got his first great opportunity at Castle Howard, through him again he received the appointment of Clerk of the Works, and through that his second great opportunity at Blenheim; other commissions, such as Seaton Delaval and King's Weston, followed naturally from that beginning; nor was Lord Carlisle content even with assisting his protégé thus far, for, though Vanbrugh's knowledge of heraldry was hardly adequate, he insisted upon his being made Clarenceux King-of-Arms; it says something for the power of a single man that he could so carry his wishes in face of opposition from almost the entire College of Heralds. Apart from the objections of other architects, which considering Vanbrugh's remarkable career may quite justifiably be a little flavoured with personal prejudice, there is no doubt that contemporary opinion was not strongly inclined to pronounce Blenheim a success. The chief objection, of course, was that the architect had abandoned the rules; Wren had been known to do that, and had not met with hostility, probably because even in his neglect of the rules there was an assurance that he knew them, while it looked remarkably as if Vanbrugh was neglecting those rules because he had never been able to learn them, much as the post-impressionist painter of 1912 used to be accused of drawing deliberately "wrong" because he could not draw "right". Those whose opinion constituted

26

Good Taste, for nearly the whole century, agreed in condemning Vanbrugh until it became a tradition to regard him with Kent (equally unjustifiably) as among the worst of the major architects. Yet Reynolds saw that there must be something great in a man whose brain could work so easily on the exalted plane of the Grand Manner; in the Thirteenth Discourse, for example, which was delivered in December 1786, after saying that one of the principal qualities held by architecture in common with painting and poetry is that of affecting the imagination by means of association of ideas, he continues: "It is from hence in a great degree that in the buildings of Vanbrugh, who was a Poet as well as an Architect, there is a greater display of imagination than we shall find perhaps in any other; and that is the ground of the effect which we feel in many of his works, notwithstanding the faults with which many of them are charged; for that purpose Vanbrugh appears to have had recourse to some principles of the Gothick Architecture. . . ." Sir Joshua devoted a good deal of time in this Thirteenth Discourse to his attempt at the re-establishment of the unfashionable Vanbrugh; he claims for him that "he had originality of invention, he understood light and shadow and had great skill in composition". After enlarging for a little on his skill in design and on his *painter-like* qualities, he then permits himself to loosen his Presidential dignity, and says with considerable warmth "he (Vanbrugh) was defrauded of the due reward of his merit by the Wits of his time, who . . . knew little or nothing of what he understood perfectly". And then, a moment later, "his fate was that of the great Perrault; both were objects of the petulant sarcasms of factious men of letters".

27

Reynolds himself suffered singularly little from men of letters, though, as must have happened to any friend of Johnson, he had seen them at their most factious; but there was another figure, no less factious and typical throughout the century, whom we may call the Important Amateur. Lord Burlington[1] and Horace Walpole are the two stock examples, but were far from being isolated phenomena; certainly until about the middle of the reign of George III it was necessary for a gentleman of quality to acquire a familiarity with the fine arts, to learn at least the names and particularities of those Italian painters most in demand or to master the rules of Palladian architecture. In these days, when the critical apparatus is so elaborate and expert knowledge so loudly proclaimed, Lord Burlington is often laughed at and even Walpole does not always escape a sneer. It may be right that the opinion of a wealthy and aristocratic amateur should not carry weight if it be not supported by any qualification other than wealth or birth, but in the society of the first two Georges, when the arts depended even more, if that is possible, than they do to-day upon the rich patron, that patron considered it as part of the obligations of his rank to have a working knowledge of what he was patronising. It was much more than the mere desire of him who pays the piper to call the tune, it was the desire of the man to whom actual creation is denied to be associated as closely as possible with the articulate, creative artist; so strong was this passion for creation, that several of these distinguished amateurs, all of whom possessed a more than superficial knowledge of the art, were led to father

[1] Richard Boyle, 3rd Earl of Burlington and 4th Earl of Cork, 1695–1753.

the designs of humbler but more skilful architects. The relations between Lord Burlington and William Kent, for example, are, though some points are disputed, in many ways an illustration of this; whatever the artistic merits or faults of either party, Burlington is clearly one of those unfortunate people whom his misguided followers and admirers have infinitely damaged; he munificently published both the *Designs of Inigo Jones* and Palladio's *Antiquities of Rome*, which with Colin Campbell's *Vitruvius Britannicus* were largely responsible for the fashion of "being interested in" architecture, a fashion of which Pope, for one, highly disapproved; "Heav'n visits with a Taste the wealthy Fool" he laughs, in the fourth of the *Moral Essays*, which he dedicates to Burlington. He continues, in the same Epistle:

> You shew us, Rome was glorious, not profuse,
> And pompous buildings once were things of Use;
> Yet shall (my Lord) your just, your noble rules
> Fill half the land with imitating fools;
> Who random drawings from your sheets shall take
> And of one beauty many blunders make;
> Load some old Church with vain Theatric state,
> Turn Arcs of Triumph to a garden-gate . . .

Pope rightly had a contempt for the unqualified amateur who tries to become master in a fortnight, but unlike the majority of great artists he had also a contempt for the amateur critic who presumes to express an opinion, which is shown in an alternative passage in the same *Moral Essay*:

> Must Bishops, Lawyers, Statesmen have the skill
> To build, to plant, judge paintings, what you will?
> Then why not Kent as well our Treaties draw,
> Bridgeman explain the Gospel, Gibbs the Law?

As occasionally happens with Pope, his indignation has

got the better of his reasoning, for while it might well be out of place for a bishop actually to build his own palace or plant his own garden, to criticise the achievements of others is not unbecoming in such distinguished personages. Nevertheless, in spite of his petulance, Pope sees the danger that lies in the "overdoing" of taste and the danger that may overtake an art when it once becomes fashionable.

Yet did not the arts, in actual fact, benefit rather than suffer when it was fashionable to be actively interested in them? What was the effect, for example, on architecture when the rich and influential "amateurs" concerned themselves with it? One of the inducements which caused so many laymen to concern themselves with architecture was, undoubtedly, the publication throughout the century, but particularly during the first half, of books of plans and designs such as Kyp and Knyff's *Noblemen's Seats* in 1709, Colin Campbell's *Vitruvius Britannicus*, which began to appear in 1715, Kent's *Inigo Jones* of 1727, Batty Langley's *Treasury of Designs* of 1740 or James Paine's *Plans and Elevations of Noblemen's Houses* of 1783; in addition to these and a great many other books of collected plans and elevations, most architects caused their patrons to publish sumptuous volumes of the plans of individual great houses when they were being built, as Matthew Brettingham had his *Plans and Sections of Holkham* published in 1761, or as the various plans for Houghton by Campbell, Ripley and Kent were brought out by Ware in 1735; behind the publication of many such volumes was the money of either Lord Burlington or Lord Pembroke.[1] It would not be to the point to discuss here the

1 Thomas Herbert, 8th Earl of Pembroke, 1656–1733.

personal achievements of either of those patrons or to what extent they appropriated the credit due to professional architects employed by them; what is to the point is that in an age of obligatory patronage they set an example of peculiar princeliness; owing to them and to the following of their example by others an immense number of great houses was set up all over England, some by architects of widespread fame such as Vanbrugh, Kent, Gibb, Ripley or Colin Campbell, others by men whose fame was local, such as Matthew Brettingham of Norfolk, Carr of York, Bell of Lynn or Wood of Bath. Against many of these great houses, built as they were, in nine cases out of ten, to rules based on Palladio, there is the objection that they were somewhat unsuited for private residences; with imposing and dignified façades, their interiors were often inconvenient, for their immense entrance halls and magnificent reception rooms meant that much else must be sacrificed. The architect, in fact, regarded the elevation as of far greater importance than the ground-plan and made everything else secondary to the façade and the "pictorial" appearance. Apparently, moreover, the patron, whoever he might be, acquiesced and was content to be condemned to a dignified discomfort. Nevertheless, the result was a dignity, a stateliness, a proportion so satisfying to look at that the majority of us are well inclined to overlook the occasional faulty application of a rule, more especially as most of us have never learnt the rules.

This existence of a fixed canon of taste, and the ability on the part of almost all educated people to describe a house as being good or bad as it accorded with the rules, ensured at least a minimum standard of excellence, so that when we say that such and such a house has faults we mean that it is not quite so good as certain other houses of its own period and style, and the very fact that it is of that period and style, that it was built between, say, 1700 and 1770, implies in itself an excellence which we can be sure is there even before we see the house. And that is perhaps the only period, except the Regency, of which this can be said. It is the fashion to laugh with Pope at "Ripley with a rule", with Walpole to condemn Kent, to dismiss Colin Campbell as a pedant or Burlington as a fraud; but before we do so, it might be salutary to consider whether nineteenth-century domestic architecture was of an excellence sufficient to justify that attitude? However uninspired was Campbell, or pompous Kent, they possessed in common with all their contemporaries a degree of scholarship which ensured that nothing they did could be actually bad, so long as they did not venture beyond the limits of their learning; when Kent, for example, made experiments in the Gothic the result was far less happy than when he confined himself to Palladio. Many foolish things have been written about the Distinguished Amateur by over-zealous admirers, which have done much to discredit them all from Burlington downwards; a good example occurs in the Rev. James Dallaway's *Observations on English Architecture*, published in 1806; discussing the architecture of Cambridge, he says, "of the original design for the senate-house Gibbs is said to have had the credit, although it was submitted to the correcting taste of Sir James Burrough". Sir James Burrough was not, as it might be thought, an architect but the Master of Caius. But that the Rev. James Dallaway was a man whose opinions are far from negligible is proved by his remarks on the Chapel

of King's at Cambridge, which, after some very perti-
nent criticisms on the exterior, he describes as being,
inside, the finest flower of late Gothic and the most
beautiful possession of either University; that is an
unusual opinion for an age which still tended to describe King's as "Gothic but very fine". It might be well,
therefore, to consider men such as Lord Burlington in
the light of another quotation from Dallaway: "Nor is
it less to be allowed, that from the great number and
accuracy of plans and elevations already published, or
from the inspection of houses completed from them, it
is practicable for a gentleman to become his own architect, leaving the inferior departments to his master-
mason". What Dallaway meant by "the inferior departments" no doubt includes the entire technical and
scientific part of building a house; at the same time this
supports the contention that the amateur had directly
as well as indirectly a good deal to do with the encouragement and improvement of the most admirable
domestic architecture that England has yet produced.

It is not, moreover, only the great country-houses
that constitute the body of this architecture; in London
and in every large or small town in England there are
simple, dignified red-brick or stone-fronted houses,
built by no named architect, figuring in no book of
County antiquities or of published Plans and Elevations; one sees them from the window of a railway
carriage or from a motor-car, but however quickly they
may have flashed past they have impressed themselves
on one, they stand out either from their quaint and
picturesque neighbours of the sixteenth or seventeenth
centuries or from the squalid vulgarity of what is the
greater part of nineteenth-century architecture. There is

about a street-frontage of the time of Queen Anne or the early Georges a simplicity and a distinction, a style, that is surpassed by no other period and rivalled perhaps only by the later Georgian or the Regency. These nameless architects, often claiming no dignity higher than that of builder, were so imbued with the principles of artistic good manners, that such matters as doors and doorsteps, the height of the frontage, the size and spacing of the windows, were dealt with by instinct; it is not necessary to assume that every builder and contractor in England was gifted divinely with perfect taste, but it may at least be said that a tradition was formed during the revival of interest in architecture at the end of the seventeenth century, which lasted about 120 years and which, though quite different from the more elaborate and exalted architecture of the same period, was yet affected by the same currents and influences and regulated in the same way, though probably unconsciously, by the varying attention paid to Taste. The taste, as we have seen, was largely picked up from the Latin countries, while some of it was imported from Holland; and here again is illustrated the double origin of the English Tradition. For while the consciously elegant productions of the fashionable architects and of the decorators for fashionable patrons proclaimed their foreign origin, the ordinary everyday work is a translation of the foreign expression into a vernacular idiom, absorbing it into the language. As our written and spoken language has borrowed from almost all Europe, from Greek and Latin, from French, Italian, German, Danish and Saxon and made therefrom its own rich self, the visual "language" of the arts has evolved by borrowing, translating and finally absorbing, as it grew, each new translation; all Europe contributed to make what finally became English, and even the Far East was drawn on. But the East proved a little too rich for the native digestion, so that *chinoiserie* remained an exotic favoured only by the fashionable, but favoured by them so highly that it forms an important chapter in the history of Taste.

CHAPTER III

CHINESE AND ROCOCO

As far back as the middle of the seventeenth century the influence of Chinese art was beginning to be felt in Europe. The Dutch merchants in the Far East were in the habit of sending home large quantities of Chinese and, though to a smaller extent, Japanese porcelain; it was a long time before this was to become in any sense popular, but amongst a few wealthy collectors in Holland and France this new ware was already highly prized; popularity did not come until certain of the great European factories began to add their own accessories to the Chinese decoration; this was quite a common practice from about 1735 until the 1750's in such centres as Dresden, Sèvres, Venice and Delft, some of which even had their own branch establishments in China; others merely imported the plain white porcelain and applied their own designs at home. As knowledge increased, naturally the finest examples were more and more sought after and valued, and elaborate ormolu mounts were devised to show them off, so elaborate, often, that the gold rococo became at least as important as the vase it was intended to support.

While the Continent was being introduced to the Orient by porcelain, England discovered its possibilities through tea. Says Pepys on 28th September 1660: "I did send for a cup of tea (a China drink) of which I

36

never had drank before". We may regret that he is so terse and matter-of-fact about it, for it would be interesting to see his nervousness over a new experiment being tempered by the conviction that he ought to be enjoying it. At any rate, many other people beside Pepys underwent this new gastronomic excitement about the same time, and tea soon became fashionable, probably because it was expensive. Naturally there proceeded from this China drink a curiosity about the people who produced it, and those with any knowledge of Chinese manners, customs, art or costume, soon found a market. The Orient, in fact, became the vogue; it had already become so in France, the first Trianon, "le Trianon de Porcelaine" (of which nothing remains), having been built in the 1670's. What was fashionable in Paris became in due course, but after something of an interval, fashionable in London, and in this particular case the Dutch influence under William and Mary and Queen Anne increased rather than mitigated this tendency to follow the French, among whom a further impetus had been given to *chinoiserie* by the genius of Watteau. He decorated the Château de la Muette with several designs based not merely on a fanciful Cathay, but also on an even more fanciful Tartary; so popular were his panels, especially after Boucher had engraved some of them, that from then till the Revolution *chinoiserie* remained perhaps the favourite of all indoor amusements amongst the fashionable.

"Un Prince est assis sous un dais d'architecture baroque, sur un riche tapis oriental, derrière lui un éléphant; devant lui des Chinois et des Indiens prosternés. Une femme arrive à gauche dans un char."

"Devant une pagode, sur les marches de laquelle est

un savant tenant une sphère, un Chinois répand des fleurs; derrière lui deux autres Chinois prosternés."

This bizarre and unexpected world existed behind a number of dignified and very English Georgian façades; a world wherein mandarins, rajahs and elephants wandered round the walls of boudoirs, among weeping-willows and pagodas. While the dignified façades, the west fronts, the south fronts, the entrance halls and the State apartments continued according to rule, some-where, it was felt, in some ante-room or bed-chamber, or some pavilion in the park, it might be permissible to be a little less English, and, having relaxed the in-sularity, to depart from the traditional and to experi-ment with something that was not included under the safe heading of "Good Taste". If one were very rich and one's house had a large number of rooms, there was no reason why one should not amuse oneself by venturing into this exciting medley of the Indies and Tartary, Africa and China, that is called *chinoiserie*. One might even go further and show off one's Chinese porcelain in a strictly Chinese room, but it was easier, on the whole, to be generally Oriental on these occasions, rather than precisely Sung or accurately T'ang. This Chinese taste was at first, and for several years, limited to decorating in this manner furniture that was of the accepted European designs, English, French or Dutch. The elaborate cabinets of lacquer and gilt that are so prominent in the reign of Charles II were made to rest on stands in the Italian or French taste; the lacquered writing-cabinets of Queen Anne, though decorated with Chinese figures and landscapes, show barely a trace of Eastern influence in their actual design any more than do the long clocks of the period (apart from certain

exceptional flights of imagination); when Chippendale
made furniture for David Garrick, he confined his
Oriental wanderings to painting green temples and
weeping-willows and pagodas on cupboards and ward-
robes that were entirely conventional in design and
that might have been made for the most conventionally-
minded patron; if the decoration were to be removed, no
trace of China would remain. On the other hand, a few
of those who preferred to try to set, rather than follow,
a fashion, took the hint given them by Sir William
Chambers[1] and had furniture specially made to Chinese
designs; they lived among dragons and temple bells, and
wore Oriental gowns over their hoops, and slept in
beds whose posts, though made of mahogany or beech,
were yet carved to look like bamboo, beneath tapering
canopies, like the tops of pagodas. And in the morning
their chocolate would be brought to them by a Chinese
boy in a pointed hat and thick-soled shoes, looking like
the one at Knole whom Reynolds painted; Chinese boys,
for a time, were almost more in demand than negroes,
though as yet neither the Blenheim spaniel nor the Italian
greyhound had been ousted by the Pekinese. Such a
room was made for the Duke of Beaufort at Badminton,
with lattice-work chairs and a bed like a temple and a
flowery wall-paper covered with parrots, herons and
blossoming shrubs.[2]

Costume, also, was affected by the taste for *chinoiserie*, though the fashion of wearing Oriental gowns
when at home in one's own house was not altogether

---

[1] See *infra*, p. 47 ff.

[2] Claydon in Buckinghamshire, a typical English house of the middle
eighteenth century, contains first-rate examples of the Etruscan, Roman,
Gothic and Chinese tastes. The Adam-Gothic and the Chippendale-
Chinese are admirably illustrated in *Country Life*, xxxi. 394.

The Rule of Taste

new; the weight and discomfort of the periwig had necessitated its being removed when indoors, but since there might be danger of taking cold some kind of cap was advisable; the turban came in. By the time of Anne, a semi-Oriental *négligé* was very fashionable; people wore, and often had themselves painted wearing, a "Moorish" turban with a Chinese, or sometimes Turkish, robe and Turkish slippers, as does Lord Sandwich in the National Portrait Gallery, as painted by Highmore in 1740. The taste for Eastern clothes spread to fancy-dress, to routs and masques; at Vauxhall, Saracens and Moors disputed for a hundred years the popularity of Punchinello or of Arlequin. But by the beginning of the nineteenth century, Greece and Albania were in higher favour than China, for the full romantic movement always preferred the Near to the Far East. But in the beginning of the pendulum's swing towards the romantic, and for many years after that beginning, the Orient captivated the fashionable mind and visitors from China or the South Seas could always depend on being lionised in London; there was that feathered and handsome Pacific Islander, Omai, who sat to Reynolds, and the Chinese Chit-qua who was painted by both Reynolds and Zoffany; Chit-qua appears in Zoffany's picture of the Life-Room of the Royal Academy, being included in that assembly ostensibly on the strength of his skill as a modeller but more probably, one cannot help feeling, because he wore Chinese dress always and had a pigtail; he became very much the fashion about 1770 and is said to have spoken excellent English, but he certainly realised that pidgin-English was expected of him and was careful not to be disappointing; he wrote, for example, to some ladies in Oxford:[1] "Some time he make voyage to Oxford, Christchurch will then open his gates and make Chit-qua so welcome he no more tinkee go Canton again; there he find much bisn, as he so well savee art of modelling Heads, thing much wanted among Mandarinmen of that place. Once more tankee fine present. Adios." How well Chit-qua knew his Oxford, although he had never been there! There is little doubt that the excited circulation of this letter among the Mandarinmen of Oxford and their ladies made his visit very well worth his while.

In the 1750's, Chippendale, seeing that imported Chinese wall-papers were beginning to decorate some of the more advanced boudoirs and bedrooms, forthwith introduced into the backs of his chairs and the galleries of his tables that lattice-work pattern that seems to form the balustrades of so many little bridges on porcelain or paper. With great dexterity he gave a Chinese flavour to some of his most intricate rococo work, and those immense mirrors, which have so seldom survived unbroken, enable us to see a strange, fabulous scene wherein macaws on palm-branches hold pomegranates in their claws, or swing from the dripping branches of willows, or fight with cranes and herons among the arabesques of limewood: the very word arabesque suggests the East. Those industrious ladies, whose mothers had covered their walnut chairs with stiff embroideries and whose daughters were to reproduce Flora's Realm with paper and scissors, themselves made involved designs in shells, coral-pink and pale yellow, representing Chinese men and Chinese women standing under temple gateways, playing busily

[1] Quoted by W. T. Whitley, *Artists and their Friends in England*, i. 270.

41

upon the flute; or recalled the willow-pattern in rolled paper.

As the century ended, so the Chinese taste began to decline; it still survived, however, in papier-mâché trays; weeping-willows gave way to dripping water, to waterfalls pouring themselves into lakes on which sail improbable boats, while herons and Buddha-like fishermen compete with one another. One of the most interesting developments of these *chinoiseries* were the *singeries*, much in vogue during the 1750's, such as Monkey Island, near Bray on the Thames, where two temples were adorned with a "monkey" *motif* for the 3rd Duke of Marlborough by the decorative artist Clermont (who was also employed by Frederick, Prince of Wales). Huet, in France, produced many of these designs, notably one still to be seen at Chantilly and described as "*les différentes actions de la vie humaine représentées par des singes*"; he shows us in these designs a very fantastic and delightful world wherein monkeys climb up and down trees and pull the tails of parrots, fling cocoanuts at flamingos, gaze at themselves in mirrors, and drink chocolate; parrots, pagodas, flamingos, Chinamen and monkeys, all are made into an elegant picture confined within a rococo frame. Sometimes, as in the Groteskensaal in the Belvedere in Vienna, a more abstract form of grotesquerie is adopted, a mere decoration of arabesques springing perhaps from a *motif* of negroes attired in feathers and crowns, or from a group of *amorini* in a corner; but this, though developing certainly from *chinoiserie*, has moved a long way from its original. The European Chinese was not by any means always fantastic, as is shown by the extremely correct Pagodenburg near Munich; here the ruler of Bavaria was in the habit of taking tea and gambling amidst Chinese surroundings that were real rather than adapted, and, since the pavilion itself is in a very modest style, the result is a little like the London house of someone who has spent his life in Hong-Kong and brought home innumerable mementoes. To be at its best in Europe, *chinoiserie* should be spiced with a suggestion of the more shameless kind of rococo, as in the descriptions quoted earlier in this chapter.

The Aubusson factory, especially in the second half of the century, took many of its ideas from Chinese subjects, as did some of the factories of *toiles* and *étoffes*, notably those at Amiens, Bourges, Richmond, Nantes and Jouy. *Toile de Jouy* is, of course, the most celebrated of these productions, with designs of the highest fantasy, where one may see dogs dancing sarabands before mandarins, butterflies tickling the noses of Emperors and pig-tailed cavaliers shooting centipedes with cannon; tempests and stormy seas are also very popular, with junks and frigates and East Indiamen all in peril together; occasionally, in their more banal moments, the designers are content with the usual groves and rocks and grottoes. An idea of some of the designs can be got from a list of "raw materials" published by Jean Pillement, which includes a "Cahier de douze Barques et Chariots Chinois",[1] a "Cahier de Parasols Chinois" and a "Livre de Chinois",[2] all described as being *très utiles pour les Manufactures des Soies*. An imitation, for those unable to afford the real *toiles*, took the form of painted or printed wall-paper. In France, at any rate, there was no limit to the extremes of fantasy; not only does one meet the more ordinary

[1] Paris, 1770.   [2] London, 1758.

Emperors, mandarins and coolies, but also Chinese shepherds and shepherdesses, and Chinese pilgrims equipped with very European staff and scrip and scallop-shell; perhaps the most unusual are a race with monkeys' heads, men's bodies and goats' legs.

In England, as for the most part in France, the Chinese taste was for many years confined to the decorations of pavilions or rooms, and as a general fashion it remained confined within the same limits. In Schönbrunn and the Belvedere, in Nymphenburg and the Huis ten Bosch, in countless Châteaux, and in Sion House, there is evidence to show how universal was the fashion and for how many years it continued; the Chinese Room of Mrs Montagu in Portman Square was one of the famous rooms of Europe. Reaction came with the severe simplicity of Greece and the Regency to abolish such extravagances of imagination. The Pavilion at Brighton is the culmination: it is the St. Martin's summer of the rococo.

While the names and the accomplishments of Thornhill, of Laguerre, of Verrio, of Angelica Kauffmann or of Cipriani are well known and eagerly sought out, those of Grace, Lambelet and Robert Jones suggest, as a rule, nothing to anybody; yet these three are responsible for the whole of the original decoration in the Pavilion;[1] for the delicate green of the entrance hall, the grey and gold of the banqueting-room, the crimson of the saloon, the crimson and blue and gold and yellow of the music-room. Sometimes they paint shadowy dragons into the graining of mahogany doors, sometimes they imitate

[1] The *Official Guide to the Pavilion*, by H. D. Roberts (edn. 1930) gives much information, and is itself founded largely on Brayley's *History of the Pavilion*, 1838. *Vide* Chapter X, *infra*.

damask, richer than any could be woven; sometimes they paint serpent-wreathed columns or flowered hangings, and sometimes visions of Pekin itself. Every trick of apparent projection, of false perspective, is theirs, and they are equally masters of splendid magnificence and subtle undertones. And it was the Regent himself who inspired them. In the last years of his regency and the first years of his reign, the domes and minarets rose under his direction, the cast-iron pillars, entwined with cast-iron serpents, sprang up to branch into palm-leaves of copper or to support a glowing Oriental sky half covered with the leaves of some huge nenuphar or a fruit-laden plantain, from whose calix hangs a golden dragon, swinging in his claws a chandelier, itself adorned with six more dragons, each holding in its mouth a lotus-flower; yet more dragons and winged serpents fly round the cornices, and from their gilded coils draped curtains hang across the windows, half obscuring the view across the Steyne. The great saloon, inadequately described as the Music Room, is the climax of the Pavilion, the climax, in fact, of *chinoiserie* in England, perhaps in Europe. From the floor to the top of the great cupola, so cunning in its deception, the eye sees nothing but a vision of a legendary China; Africa and Hindustan are banished, and Pekin is borne by dragons from mirror to mirror round the walls.

If this be the St. Martin's summer of the rococo, the high summer was, as it tends to be among the English seasons, short; it produced nevertheless one splendid rose at least, the State Coach; this, perhaps the finest single piece of rococo made in England, built for the Coronation of George III, was designed by Sir William Chambers, with Cipriani and Wilton to assist him; the master of the Kew Pagoda thus redeems English rococo from being wholly negligible, even though the pedantic might object, with Horace Walpole, to the conjunction of such aquatic tritons with such terrestrial palm-trees.

While those who are sufficiently wealthy are at liberty to adorn the interiors of their houses in any manner that fashion or their own tastes may dictate, the architect, as opposed to the decorator, must appeal to a larger audience; not much larger, perhaps, because the number of people who ever notice architecture at all is limited. To introduce a new style that is altogether alien to that prevailing at the moment, in a manner that will alter the outward appearance of a place, has always been difficult in England from the age of Queen Anne onwards; and the introduction of the Oriental into architecture on anything except the smallest scale met with so little encouragement that very few architects seriously attempted it; one of those who did was William Halfpenny, between 1749 and 1753, and his only recognition has been to be bracketed in polite derision with Batty Langley as a well-meaning seeker after novelty;[1] and in 1753 some builder whose name is now forgotten threw across the Thames at Hampton Court a slender, switch-backed bridge of seven arches which, in the following year, was drawn by Canaletto and not long after that was demolished. By far the most important attempt to popularise the

[1] A selection of Halfpenny's publications, 1749–52, shows the earnestness of his attempts to marry the new romanticism of the "Cottage Ornée" with the even newer romanticism of the pagoda: *Twelve Beautiful Designs for Farm-Houses; New Designs for Chinese Temples; Thirteen new Designs for Parsonages and Farm-Houses; Rural Architecture in the Gothic Taste; Rural Architecture in the Chinese Taste; Chinese and Gothic Architecture Properly Ornamented.*

taste was that of the great Sir William Chambers. "Great" is not too emphatic an adjective to apply to an artist who could adapt his genius to the immense scale of Somerset House and to the intimacy of the Albany. But long before these classic experiments were made, Chambers had been to China, for he visited Canton when he was twenty. The native buildings, costumes and furniture pleased him greatly, and he filled many note-books with sketches of them for no reason other than that they did please him; he did not return straight to England, but spent some years studying in Italy and France, and when he settled in London it is probable that his mind was more full of Palladio and Bernini, of Mansard and Fischer von Erlach than of Canton. But the Chinese note-books were not forgotten, and when he was given his first big commission, out they came; this was to lay out the gardens of Kew for the Dowager Princess of Wales, mother of the young man who was in a year or two, in 1760, to become George III. The gardens were laid out, in the main, according to the approved standards of the late 1750's, and the majority of the little Temples and Pavilions were in the best and most restrained classic manner, from the exquisite Orangery to the little round-topped affair on the hill where the cranes live among the daffodils; but the impulse to experiment could not be resisted, the impulse to try to do something not quite ordinary. The memories of Canton had never faded, and now that he was given a free hand, he grasped the opportunity to carry out an experiment he had thought of ten years earlier. The result was the Pagoda. It was not due entirely to a desire to be unusual, for he believed that Chinese buildings could be very suitable in certain

European surroundings; not, certainly, for habitation, but as *divertissements* in gardens. Obviously he was uncertain as to the reception his Pagoda would meet with, for, as he observes, hoping that it would support him against the inevitable attacks of those who resented the public exhibition of what had hitherto been the private amusement of a few, "several of my good friends have endeavoured to dissuade me from publishing this work,[1] through a persuasion that it would hurt my reputation as an Architect; and I pay so much deference to their opinion that I would certainly have desisted had it not been too far advanced before I knew their sentiments: yet I cannot conceive why it should be criminal in a traveller to give an account of what he has seen worthy of notice in China, any more than in Italy, France or any other country; nor do I think it possible that any man should be so void of reason as to infer that an Architect is ignorant in his profession, merely from his having published designs of Chinese buildings." Probably he had in mind a remark made by Hogarth[2] about five years earlier: "There is at present such a thirst after variety that even paltry imitations of Chinese buildings have a kind of vogue, chiefly on account of their novelty". The anticipated attacks came, his defence failed, and Chambers gave up *chinoiserie* for ever. Perhaps he was wise; Somerset House at any rate justifies his decision. There is in most successful *chinoiserie* something akin to wit, which flourishes best in dining-rooms or drawing-rooms; and architecture is not a drawing-room art.

The Classic styles persisted through the century largely by reason of the age's love of good manners,

[1] *Designs of Chinese Buildings, etc.. 1757.*
[2] *Analysis of Beauty, 1753, p. 45.*

and a country-house, a church or a park of the 1740's or the 1760's, even if pompous, is always well-mannered. But perfect manners sometimes become a little tedious, and at intervals during the century these attempts were made to escape into an atmosphere less rarefied: both the Gothic and the Oriental tastes sprang partly from this desire, as reactions against the tyranny of regularity. But these very reactions were bound to be modified by that horror of barbarism that makes the period so highly civilised; Nature, left to herself, was barbaric; the Middle Ages were barbaric; the East was barbaric; if these were to be drawn upon and made to serve society, they must be controlled, disciplined and regularised. "Capability" Brown regularised Nature and gave her some superficial resemblance to art; Wyatt regularised the Gothic. But the Chinese could only re-main Chinese, and so far as it persisted at all it did so either as an amusement or as a museum exhibit.

If the Chinese and the Gothic tastes are well-con-trolled reactions against the Classic order, so also must be the taste for Ruins and for Grottoes built, arranged or excavated to provide a refuge or a view; either might be the setting for a Gothic novel, a meditation or a tea-party. *Chinoiserie* may imply fantasy and rococo wit; but infection with the Orient, however westernised, may also imply the germ of mystery, and mystery depends on terror.

At Oatlands, near London, there is a small ruin, built about the middle of the eighteenth century in the medieval taste, hidden beyond the tennis courts, the swimming-pools and the terraced gardens of an hotel and surrounded by brambles and ivy; a muddy little path slopes down to an iron gate on one side and on the further side a few steps ascend to another iron gate. This upper entrance leads into a circular chamber with a domed roof, into which the light penetrates through lunettes filled with painted glass. The walls of this chamber are entirely covered with pieces of marble, glass, blue-john, spar and quartz, inset here and there with tiny convex mirrors; great pieces of coral branch out at intervals and stalactites, encrusted like the walls, hang from above; the daylight, diffused through the small coloured windows, or the rays of one's torch, flash back in turn from each segment of the circle; it was for such rooms as this that Chippendale designed chairs and settees in the likeness of open oysters or mussels, and tables with tops like flat rocks on supports like coral, all painted and varnished to reflect the reflected light. From the lower entrance a passage twists and doubles, so that all sense of distance is lost, leading at length into another circular chamber, whose walls and roof are contrived to look more like rock than any cavern; here, in this two-storied grotto, where everything is counterfeit, the ruin built and the weeds planted, the "rock" fixed to the walls and the "stalactites" to the rock, is gay and elaborately elegant rococo with, nevertheless, a touch of pedantry in the mineralogical flavour of the upper chamber.

At West Wycombe, in Buckinghamshire, stands the famous mausoleum built for Sir Francis Dashwood, George Bubb Dodington and other members of the Hell-Fire Club, adjacent to the lovely church, crowning an abrupt, grass-covered hill and itself crowned with a golden globe. Conscientious in his duty towards the Club, Dashwood ensured its members a fitting scene for their rites by burrowing into the hill and hollowing out a great banqueting-hall beneath the altar of the church; pleased with his position as a local landowner, he found an agreeable method of disposing of the many tons of hill so excavated by dressing his fields with them.[1] At the foot of the slope is a grey-flint ruin in the monastic style, like the west front of a dismantled abbey-church; a doorway leads into a corridor which continues for some quarter of a mile, branching off at intervals into the blackness, sloping a little downwards, sometimes changing, apparently, its direction, and always without any light from outside; the floor is rough and muddy, the walls wholly unadorned; the great central chamber, with its vaulted roof, is like a natural cavern round which have been cut at intervals pointed archways leading again into the dark; and beyond, many yards further into the hill, is the last, small apartment in which so many of the beguiled village maids ceased to be maids. There is no gaiety, no elegance here; it might be the crypt of the not very distant Medmenham Abbey; it might still be haunted by the black monkey secretly released by Wilkes when Lord Sandwich invoked the Devil; it might inspire a Collins, a Gray or a Blair to his graveyard contemplations. There is darkness and Gothic terror, increased rather than dispelled by the thought of the banquets beneath the altar, when torches deepened the shadows and the wine was drunk from skulls.

[1] This relationship between Dashwood's pleasures and duties was suggested by an architect friend of the author.

CHAPTER IV

SUBLIME AND PICTURESQUE

PERHAPS one of the reasons why the taste for *chinoiserie* never spread very wide is the impossibility of establishing a canon of the fantastic, so that while the Man of Taste permitted himself in his grottoes and his drawing-rooms an occasional departure he could not long deprive himself of the security of the rules; or perhaps it is that the rules were there and that he could not escape them, whether he would or no. We have seen these rules being formulated and observed in the creative arts, in painting and architecture especially; in the art of seeing and perceiving rules also were found necessary for guidance, and were accordingly laid down by the persons of authority and dutifully observed by the right-minded, with the result that by the end of the eighteenth century appreciation of natural beauties was an essential in any person claiming to be so minded; to lack this appreciation was to lack sensibility, and that, as Jane Austen makes clear, was to be *demodé*. The very enthusiasm with which people pointed out to one another the beauties of the natural scene shows how recent was the realisation of such beauties; it was, in fact, scarcely more than a hundred years old and had developed, consciously, during the century.

The later seventeenth century had possessed a scientific temper, more interested in trying to find out the reasons for things than in the actual appearance and form of those things; and side by side with the Scientific marched the Moral. When travellers wrote home from France, Germany or Italy, they would describe the moral effect on themselves of such scenery as they happened to notice (if they described it at all), but would very soon round off that part with some appropriate reflection, and devote the rest of their space to descriptions of some of the countless ingenuities in which seventeenth-century men of science were so prolific; an occasional traveller, such as an Evelyn, will describe works of art or antiquities; but of the ability to appreciate the "view" for its own sake there is hardly a hint, and what hints there are come on one as a surprise, as does the intrusion of an English word in a foreign language.

The sixteenth century, apart from a few of the Elizabethan poets, had had no more eye for Nature than the fifteenth or the fourteenth (Chaucer, in this as in almost every other respect, is exceptional), but even the Tudors had to take some notice of Nature when, for example, it came to laying out a garden. Great palaces such as Hampton Court or Nonesuch could not be considered complete until the ground immediately surrounding them had been brought into some sort of relation with the building itself; the fantastic, twisted chimneys and too elaborate ornament, all the architectural conceits, had their exact counterpart in the intricate knot-gardens and mazes, the arbours and alleys and fanciful sundials, the cunningly contrived fountains and waterworks that spurted suddenly into life through the action of a hidden spring; with, in addition to all these, a bowling alley, an orchard, a physick garden, a fishpond and a great many leaden statues and ornamental tanks the "sweet simplicity of the old-world garden" was complete. The whole of this type of garden, or rather series of small gardens, was surrounded by a brick wall, beyond which might be a forest, a chace, a deer-park or the open countryside, but in any case there was a clearly marked demarcation between the pleasure-ground belonging to the house and the land beyond. This demarcation remained almost universal in England, and indeed elsewhere, till about the second quarter of the eighteenth century, though the arrangement of the garden itself began to show a change after the Restoration.

This change that came over the English gardens after 1660 was due, like most other changes about that time, to French influence. Lenôtre had been laying out the great gardens of France in a patterned smoothness like so many Aubusson carpets, and every English owner of a country-house conceived the ambition to emulate Versailles or St. Germains; the older type of garden still lingered on here and there to the end of the century, but by the reign of Queen Anne the revolution was accomplished. Flowers to all intents and purposes had been banished; the house was surrounded now by broad terraces and smooth stretches of lawn, and from it radiated, for miles, great avenues of lime and chestnut; instead of fishponds there were canals, parterres in place of knot-gardens, and, perhaps the most important change, the garden was no longer separated so distinctly from the park. A very good idea of the splendid formal garden of William and Mary or Anne is given by Kyp's "Views" published in *Britannia Illustrata,* or by *Les Délices de la Grande Bretagne*, or by Atkyns's *Gloucestershire* or by any of the other great folios of engravings published at this time, similar to those dealing with the plans and elevations of the houses themselves. For architecture and formal gardening were becoming polite accomplishments; every gentleman liked to think himself capable, after the study of *Vitruvius Britannicus* and *Britannia Illustrata*, master of the laws of Palladio and Lenôtre and capable of building his own house and laying out his own garden. The two arts had been revolutionised along very similar lines; as the house was regarded as a complete and homogeneous work of art, so too was its garden, and the scholarship and science of the Italian were joined to the scholarship and science of the Frenchman to produce a work of art in which house and garden played equal parts. The Palladian architects insisted that the laying out of the grounds should be complementary to their own work; they may have sacrificed much to their façade, but at least they insured that the façade should have a worthy setting and that the approaches to it should convey a preliminary idea of the splendours at the end. Wren intended that Hampton Court should be approached by the great avenue at Bushey.

Yet another change, however, began to make its appearance about the 1720's, and an even greater change than any that had yet come about; while hitherto gardens had passed from small-scale formality to formality on a scale almost monumental, they now began to move from that formality towards an equally studied informality. The truth of the matter is that Nature, provided that she behaved herself, was coming into fashion and the countryside was beginning to be noticed; it was hardly possible to extend the garden and the park any more, so as to include all the visible country beyond, but it was at least possible to create an illusion of so doing by removing the conspicuous barriers and substituting a demarcation that was, from the immediate neighbourhood of the house, invisible. This process can still be best described by quoting[1] Horace Walpole's well-known remarks. After condemning the sixteenth- and seventeenth-century formal gardens, he praises Charles Bridgeman for having begun the reformation that indicated the dawn of modern taste, in that he "enlarged his plans, disdained to make every part tally to its opposite". The taste for "natural" gardens had begun, but still there remained the obstacle of the enclosing wall or hedge; and then, at last, "the capital stroke, the leading step to all that has followed, was the destruction of walls as boundaries and the invention of fosses—an attempt then deemed so astonishing that the common people called them Ha-Ha's to express their surprise at finding a sudden and unperceived check to their walk". Whatever the degree of accuracy in Horace Walpole's derivation of ha-ha, it is probably the most important single innovation in the whole history of gardens; with the removal of the barrier the artificial formality must go too, and instead of the garden being made to harmonise with the house it must be made to harmonise with the whole surrounding view; "adieu", said Walpole, "to the canals, circular basins, cascades tumbling down marble steps". Henceforth, though "Capability" Brown might disapprove of Kent, and Uvedale Price pour scorn on "Capability" and Humphrey Repton differ politely from Uvedale Price and all disagree with Walpole, the points of disagreement seem to us, a century and a half re-

[1] Horace Walpole, *Treatise on Modern Gardening. Collected Works*, vol. ii.

moved, comparatively unimportant; what really matters is that, since formality had gone as far as scholarship and a sense of magnitude could take it, taste abruptly changed. If, as Horace Walpole said, Kent leapt the fence out of the old garden, it might almost equally be said that Nature herself leapt the same fence into the garden. Kent, and after him Brown, laid out their gardens on strictly landscape lines. "Clumps" were planted to break the level uniformity of lawns, and canals were banished in favour of purling streams, taught to meander and to serpentine; ruins were constructed, and grottoes and artificial rocks. With all this "naturalness" and "picturesqueness", a typical English garden in the middle of the century could still contain, within the space of a few acres, a Greek temple, a Palladian bridge, a Gothic summer-house, a Roman ruin and a Chinese pagoda. The *jardin anglais* had come into being, remote and half-forgotten ancestor of those countless arid patches in modern Italian towns dignified by the description of "*Giardino inglese*". But the *jardin anglais* of the eighteenth century was often called also *jardin chinois*; so nearly interchangeable are the terms that Sir William Chambers's description of a Chinese garden[1] may serve for the description of the fashionable English ideal; it is worth quoting at some length.

"Their artists", he says, "distinguish three different species of scenes, to which they give the appellations of pleasing, horrid and enchanted. Their enchanted scenes answer in a great measure to what we call romantic, and in these they make use of several artifices to excite

---

[1] Sir Wm. Chambers's *Designs of Chinese Buildings, etc.*, 1757. This is some fifteen years earlier than his larger *Dissertation on Oriental Gardening*.

57

surprise. Sometimes they make a rapid stream or torrent pass underground, the turbulent noise of which strikes the ear of the newcomer, who is at a loss to know whence it proceeds; at other times they dispose the rocks, buildings and other objects that form the composition in such a manner as that the wind passing through the different interstices and cavities, made in them for that purpose, causes strange and uncommon sounds. They introduce into these scenes all kinds of extraordinary trees, plants and flowers, form artificial and complicated echoes and let loose different sorts of monstrous birds and animals. In their scenes of horror they introduce impending rocks, dark caverns and impetuous cataracts rushing down the mountains from all sides; the trees are ill-formed and seemingly torn to pieces by the violence of tempests; some are thrown down and intercept the course of the torrents appearing as if they had been brought down by the fury of the waters; others look as if shattered and blasted by the force of the lightning; the buildings are some in ruins, others half consumed by fire, and some miserable huts dispersed in the mountains serve at once to indicate the existence and wretchedness of the inhabitants. These scenes are generally succeeded by pleasing ones."

The rest of Chambers's description is equally vivid and instructive; he enlarges on their use of contrast, describes how in their gardens one passes "from limited prospects to extensive views, from objects of horror to scenes of delight"; how they have different scenes contrived for morning, noon and evening; how fond they are of an extensive use of water, in the form of lakes and rivers and cascades and so forth; he mentions their use of artificial rocks, covered with moss and briar and

topped by little temples with rugged steps ascending
to them; and, their supreme ingenuity, a forced perspective, giving an idea of space and recession in a small
garden by making buildings actually smaller as they were
most distant and colouring them in a greyish tinge. In
the distance also trees and shrubs were planted "of a
fainter colour and a smaller growth". All this may be,
and doubtless is, based on Chambers's recollections of
the few gardens he was able to see in China, but it is
also what he hoped all English gardens would soon
become and was certainly published to that end; nor
was it published altogether without success, so that
even Horace Walpole found the fashion for picturesque
gardens a trifle excessive and out of place. "They talk",
he complained,[1] "of purling streams and shady groves,
and all we get is sore throats and influenza." Pagodas and
other garden *chinoiseries* were fashionable with a few
people for a short time, but the picturesque garden, the
jardin anglais or *chinois*, had come and was to remain.
Taste, though exercising a sovereignty as despotic as
ever, was moving in all the arts away from the earlier
rules laid down by prescribed masters and substituting
a new set for the old; architecture in the second half
of the eighteenth century was beginning to abandon
Palladio; poetry was forgetting Pope and Dryden; painting was leaving the High for the Late Renaissance;
though Sublimity, Beauty and Grace were not dead, and
neither Burke nor Hogarth forgotten, picturesqueness
for the time was the only mode.

One must agree with Sir Uvedale Price[2] that "there
are few words whose meaning has been less accurately

---

[1] Horace Walpole, *Letters*.
[2] Uvedale Price, *Essay on the Picturesque*.

determined than that of the word Picturesque". He, more than anyone else, is responsible for the introduction and use of the word in its strictly specialised meaning; that is to say, not in the loose and general way in which the adjective is applied to-day to anything considered fit to make a picture, but with the narrower implication of actually resembling art; he was careful to derive it from *pittore*, a painter, rather than from *pittura*, a picture, and used it of scenes or groups of objects which were composed by man or Nature in accordance with the laws of art, and, since it was the end of the eighteenth century, of romantic rather than classic art. To determine the exact meaning of this newly invented Picturesque quality it was necessary first to determine what it was *not*; this was comparatively easy, for the substantive adjectives applicable to works of art or Nature hitherto in use were not many and were all clearly defined; to students of aesthetics such as the young Edmund Burke, the Horrid, the Sublime and the Great implied certain clearly understood qualities, while the Beautiful implied certain quite different and equally well-understood qualities. In his famous treatise[1] Burke at great length, and with overmuch labouring of somewhat obvious points, defined first the one and then the other; after which Uvedale Price gave a "skeleton analysis" of Burke. Many earlier writers, from Jonathan Richardson onwards, had devoted themselves to the same subjects, with the result that, however loosely we may use those adjectives to-day, there is little doubt of the manner in which the eighteenth century used "sublime" and "beautiful".

Richardson, to begin with, emphasises the implica-

---

[1] *On the Sublime and Beautiful,* 1756.

tion, by the word Sublime, of *immensity*; "to be sublime the thought must be great: what is mean and trifling is incapable of it. There must be something that fills the mind, and that with dignity."[1] Burke also insists on this when he says "sublime objects are vast in their dimensions, beautiful ones comparatively small". But to Burke, as to Price, the primary quality of the Sublime is the capacity to arouse terror or such associated ideas as those of pain, danger and (to our ears an abrupt descent) astonishment; astonishment implies for him a degree of *horror*, "astonishment is the effect of the sublime in its highest degree; the inferior effects are admiration, reverence and respect". With the critic's love of precise classification, Burke groups all the emotions under the two headings of what he calls the chief human instincts, those of self-preservation and self-propagation; terror suggests the Sublime and love the Beautiful. Perhaps this is as reasonable a distinction as any could be, and has at any rate more originality than Price's platitude, "beauty is in one sense a collective idea and includes the sublime as well as the picturesque; in the other, it is confined to particular qualities, which distinguish it from the other two characters", for Burke never admits the collective sense of either of his two adjectives; in fact, he makes perfectly clear precisely what he does mean: "Sublime objects are vast in their dimensions; beautiful ones comparatively small; beauty should be smooth and polished; the great, rugged and negligent; beauty should shun the right line, yet deviate from it insensibly; the great in many cases loves the right line, and when it deviates, makes a strong deviation; beauty should not be obscure; the great ought

1 *Theory of Painting.*

61

to be dark and gloomy; beauty should be light and delicate; the great ought to be solid and even massive". To many this was too precise a definition, especially of the Beautiful, for not everyone had, or has, Burke's nice sense of epithet. Price had quarrelled with the practices of "Capability" Brown, but they were at one in their disapproval of the old formal gardeners whose inspiration was neither Nature nor painting, but architecture. But even though he disagreed with Brown and Kent and the other improvers, he felt it necessary to respect them, to some extent, as reformers who by their courage and enthusiasm broke down old narrow prejudices; yet, while in one hand offering the tribute of his praise, with the other he snatched it away by accusing them of demolishing without distinction the "costly and magnificent decorations of past times". The eighteenth century is not generally credited with reverence for the past, with respect for or even much interest in the works of its predecessors; it is perhaps not unexpected that the chief impression made on Price by the great formal gardens of the seventeenth century was of their evident costliness; what really mattered was that, though such gardens showed a deplorable, old-fashioned taste, they were at least made by men with a proper respect for rank and wealth. That was a point emphasised by Repton, too, who insisted that a gentleman in laying out his grounds should make the most of the *approach*, which ought to leave the highway, not at a sudden right-angle, but at a bend visible for some distance along the road; the lodge gates should always dominate that part of the village in the immediate neighbourhood, because everything must be subordinate to the gates and the park, and "a few miserable cottages" could always be pulled down and rebuilt, if necessary, in a proper manner.[1]

When, in the reaction from rigid formalisation, the improvers during two-thirds of the eighteenth century preached their successive gospels, one finds the difference coming to a head with Price's declaration of his position. "It is my wish", he says,[2] "that a more liberal and extended use of improvement should prevail; that instead of the narrow mechanical practice of a few English gardens, the noble and varied works of the eminent painters of every age and every country, and those of their supreme mistress Nature, should be the great models of imitation". By the publication of *A Letter to Uvedale Price*, by Humphrey Repton, and Price's reply, opinion was divided; everyone agreed that a new mode for gardens was desirable, but no one was agreed on what the new mode should be. It was then that Uvedale Price invented the new classification of Picturesque; briefly, this implies a certain roughness in place of the "tender smoothness" of the Beautiful, and all the abruptness of the Sublime without its overwhelming greatness; "the two opposite qualities", he says, "of roughness and of sudden variation, joined to that of irregularity, are the most efficient causes of the Picturesque". These qualities, he admits, are more often to be met with in art than in natural objects, in which he agrees with the Rev. William Gilpin, after himself the greatest authority on the Picturesque, and regrets with him "that there are so few perfect compositions in nature". Almost on the same page, however, he utters

---

[1] Humphrey Repton, *Observations on the Theory and Practice of Landscape Gardening*, 1803.
[2] Uvedale Price, *Essay on the Picturesque*, 1794.

a warning to the sentimentalist, who may imagine that rubbish in decay is picturesque, in saying that "filthy objects are often Picturesque, but not because they are filthy", and again, "I do not mean to infer that an object to be Picturesque must be old and decayed, but that the most Beautiful objects will become so from the effects of age and decay". More than once Price betrays a certain lack of confidence in his own theories that Burke never has, as, for example, when he concedes that the Picturesque may not always be applicable to modern gardening but adds defiantly "the principles of painting are always so"; Price thus stresses the part played in its composition by painters and painting, while Repton tends to dismiss that as almost unimportant; he concedes, it is true, something in expressing his opinion that "*painting* and *gardening* are nearly connected, but not so intimately as you imagine; they are not sister arts proceeding from the same stock, but rather congenial natures brought together like man and wife".[1] An important light is thrown on the eighteenth-century vocabulary in Repton's distinction between a *landscape* and a *prospect*, a point which is not taken up by his opponent and which has been, unfortunately, generally lost sight of to-day; he defines a Landscape as being the proper subject for a painter and a Prospect as that in which everybody delights. It would not be exaggerating to say that in all this celebrated argument no point is made clear by either party of greater importance than this; is not the whole question of the relationship between Art and Nature based on this distinction?

Price replies to Repton's attack point by point

[1] Humphrey Repton, *A Letter to Uvedale Price, Esq.*

64

(with that one important exception) with a great deal of rather fatiguing redundancy; even Repton's frivolous suggestion that if the painters' landscape be really indispensable to the perfection of gardening it would surely be better to paint it on canvas and hang it at the end of an avenue (as, he alleges, they do in Holland) Price answers with unbending solemnity. He is exacting, for he demands that he who would lay out his grounds (which he is careful to differentiate from the garden) in a truly picturesque manner must not only study and master the principles of painting but must be prepared to sacrifice much of his comfort; "in all this", he reminds his reader, "convenience and propriety are not the objects of consideration"; he will not admit that they have much to do with that "refined and delicate sense called taste"; the owner must not learn so much how to care for his grounds as how to neglect them, for an appearance of splendid confusion and romantic decay, enhanced by a ruin, is an important constituent of the Picturesque; gravel walks, for instance, though doubtless dry underfoot, are inadvisable, for, he says, "symmetry and regularity are particularly adverse to the picturesque". This explains the importance attached by worshippers of the Picturesque to Gothistic architecture, since the Gothic seemed asymmetrical when compared with the rectilinear buildings of the Palladian and Grecian styles; consider Repton's habit of contrasting a Gothic building with "round-headed" trees and a classic house with conical firs; he never combined pinnacle with pinnacle or the regular with the regular. From the same cause springs the delight in ruins; Price considered a ruin to be more picturesque than a new and complete building by reason of the destruction of symmetry; yet while he advocates the building of ruins, he condemns Kent for his planting of dead trees. The finding of pleasure in decay is a complex question, and not unfamiliar to us, who know those who admire a tumble-down cottage chiefly because it is tumbling down and will endure any discomfort to secure a convincingly "old world" and "quaint" atmosphere. Easier to sympathise with, perhaps, are those who see the past reflected in a present ruin, the indefatigable conjurers of ghosts. To such Marius in exile is always more impressive than Marius in power.

Even Horace Walpole studied the new Picturesque taste with as much earnestness and discrimination as he gave to the Gothic; in his *Journals of Visits to Country Seats* [1] he is always critical of whatever examples he may find. In 1770, for example, he visits Bulstrode and notes "in the park a cave in fine taste, designed by Mrs Delaney"; and in the following year he is at Lord Kent's, at Wrest, where "the Gardens are fine and very ugly in the old-fashioned manner, with high hedges and canals, at the end of the principal one of which is a frightful temple designed by Mr Archer, the groom-porter. Mr Brown has much corrected this garden, and built a Hermitage and cold bath in a bold, good taste." Elsewhere in the same journal he gives a description, too long to quote, of a Picturesque grotto, cave, temple and garden.

Returning, for a moment, to Edmund Burke and his mid-century definition of the Beautiful, we find two important points on which he disagrees surprisingly with almost every critic from Hogarth onwards; one is

[1] Walpole Society, vol. xvi.

the efficacy of the exact canons of proportion, generally so firmly believed in during the eighteenth century, and the other the beauty (in its wide modern sense) of anything that is peculiarly fitted to its purpose, a beauty often exaggerated by modern worshippers of machinery. As the century grew older the worship of the Antique increased; those statues of the Antinous or of Venus that were by common consent the most admirable works of antiquity came to be regarded as the sole criterion, so that eclectics believed in the possibility of creating Ideal Beauty by the comparatively simple process of studying the proportions of such statues and repeating them; so widespread was this comfortable belief that Burke's pronouncement is not, as it may perhaps seem to us, a labouring of the obvious; "deformity", he says, "arises from the want of the common proportions; but the necessary result of their existence in any object is not beauty"; a remark in no way heeded by the eclectics, who continued to pursue the Ideal. When Burke is attacking the other equally widespread belief that an object well fitted to a particular purpose is necessarily beautiful, he quotes, in a dignified and stately manner, various zoological phenomena, as, for examples, the great bill of the pelican and the trunk of the elephant, which, though doubtless well suited to those creatures' habits, are not, in our eyes, beautiful. The hedgehog is quoted also by him, for if efficiency were synonymous with beauty then that animal "so well secured against all assaults by his prickly hide" and the porcupine "with his missile quills" would be considered as creatures of no small elegance.

The porcupine is also quoted by Uvedale Price, when he is attempting to define the Picturesque; when "the bristles on the chafed and foaming boar, the quills on the fretful porcupine, are raised by sudden emotion", such marks of rage and fierceness are picturesque. Undoubtedly they fulfil some of the conditions, as there is a certain roughness and abruptness, a wild disorder, about such manifestations. Price also cites many of the more domesticated animals, in order to emphasise his distinction between the Picturesque and the Beautiful; the ass, he maintains, is more picturesque than the horse, the Pomeranian or rough water-dog than the smooth spaniel or the greyhound, the shaggy goat than the sheep; the sheep, in fact, answers very well to the Beautiful, since, not only has it an "innocent character so suited to the pastoral scenes of which they are the natural inhabitants", but it also possesses "a tint at once brilliant and mellow, which unites happily with all objects".

Sir Joshua Reynolds, in a letter to William Gilpin, written towards the end of his life,[1] suggests definitions which, though they may imply further definition and though not everybody may agree on the aptness of his illustration, are of importance as coming from him; his eyesight was failing, but his mind was as active and his judgments as clearly expressed as they had been when the Discourses were being pronounced. "Though I read now but little, yet I have read with great attention the essay which you was so good as to put into my hands, on the difference between the *beautiful* and the *picturesque*; and I may truly say I have received much pleasure and improvement. Without opposing any of your sentiments, it has suggested an idea that may be

[1] 19th April 1791. Quoted in *Letters of Sir Joshua Reynolds*, ed. Frederick Whiley Hilles, 1929.

worth consideration whether the epithet *picturesque* is not applicable to the excellences of the inferior schools rather than to the higher. The works of Michael Angelo, Raphael, etc., appear to me to have nothing of it; whereas Reubens and the Venetian painters may almost be said to have nothing else. Perhaps *picturesque* is somewhat synonymous to the word *taste*, which we should think improperly applied to Homer and Milton, but very well to Pope or Prior. I suspect that the application of these words are to excellences of an inferior order, and which are incompatible with the grand stile. You are certainly right in saying that variety of tints and forms is picturesque; but it must be remembered, on the other hand, that the reverse of this (uniformity of colour and a long continuation of lines) produces grandeur."

Sir Joshua was neither an industrious nor a skilful correspondent, but this letter is perhaps the most illuminating that he wrote, by reason of the light it throws on an intellect equal to, and typical of, the best minds of his age; we are perhaps shocked by his ranking Rubens and Titian below Raphael or promoting Prior to the level of Pope, but we can at least assure ourselves that if Reynolds placed them thus the weightiest opinion of his day thus, too, placed them.

Finally, by way of contrast, what may be called the opposition view to those of Payne Knight, Uvedale Price and Humphrey Repton is presented, without extreme exaggeration, by Thomas Love Peacock in *Headlong Hall*, published in 1816; to quote passages of so well known a work might seem superfluous, yet it may at least serve the purpose of recalling to memory the figure of Mr Milestone, "a picturesque landscape gardener of the first celebrity", who, it is generally agreed, is a portrait of Payne Knight.

Immediately after his arrival at Headlong Hall, Mr Milestone showed himself "impatient to take a walk round the grounds, that he might examine how far the system of clumping and levelling could be carried advantageously into effect". After he had walked a few paces, "I perceive", said Mr Milestone, "these grounds have never been touched by the finger of taste . . . my dear sir, accord me your permission to wave the wand of enchantment over your grounds. The rocks shall be blown up, the trees shall be cut down, the wilderness and all its goats shall vanish like mist. Pagodas and Chinese bridges, gravel walks and shrubberies, bowling-greens, canals and clumps of larch shall rise upon its ruins."

Before long, Mr Milestone had produced his portfolio in order to point out the beauties of his plans for Lord Littlebrain's park, and the following conversation ensued:

"MR MILESTONE. This, you perceive, is the natural state of one part of the grounds. Here is a wood, never yet touched by finger of taste, thick, intricate and gloomy. Here is a little stream, dashing from stone to stone, and overshadowed by these untrimmed boughs.

"MISS TENORINA. The sweet romantic spot! . . .

"MISS GRAZIOSA. Dear sister! how can you endure the horrid thicket?

"MR MILESTONE. You are right, Miss Graziosa: your taste is correct—perfectly *en règle*. Now here is the same place corrected—trimmed—polished—decorated —adorned. Here sweeps a plantation, in that beautiful regular curve: there winds a gravel walk: here are parts of the old wood, left in these majestic circular clumps, disposed at equal distances with wonderful symmetry . . . here is another part of the grounds in its natural state; here is a large rock, with the mountain ash rooted in its fissures, overgrown, as you see, with ivy and moss; and from this part of it bursts a little fountain, that runs bubbling down its rugged sides.

"MISS TENORINA. O how beautiful! How I should love the melody of that miniature cascade!

"MR MILESTONE. Beautiful, Miss Tenorina! Base, common and popular. . . . Now, observe the metamorphosis; here is the same rock, cut into the shape of a giant; in one hand he holds a horn, through which that little fountain is thrown to a prodigious elevation. In the other is a ponderous stone, so exactly balanced as to be apparently ready to fall on the head of any person who may happen to be beneath; and there is Lord Littlebrain walking under it."

And so it continues, with everything admired by the unsophisticated Miss Tenorina dismissed by Mr Milestone as bad taste, and with several footnotes referring the reader to Knight on *The Landscape* or to Knight on *Taste*. Nor was Peacock the only enemy of the school, as is made clear by Farington,[1] writing in the same year, 1816: "Owen spoke of the great loss which the Royal Academy and the arts in general had suffered by the death of Sir Joshua Reynolds. Opinion was so much in favour of his taste and judgment that had he lived it would have been impossible for Mr Payne Knight and the other members of the Committee of Taste to have obtained the importance they have done, and that they should be referred to for decisions as they now are."

[1] *Diary*, viii. 53.

CHAPTER V

STRAWBERRY HILL AND FONTHILL

THE raptures of Miss Tenorina were actually more *en
règle* than the projects of Mr Milestone, for by 1816
the improvements of Brown and Knight were no longer
fashionable and Peacock was trying to kill a taste already
dead, in England at least; for since the conventions
governing the art of seeing had laid it down that romantic scenery was to be admired, Miss Tenorina was
perfectly correct in doing so; there were certainly still
Mr Milestones who preferred the cultivated picturesque
to the uncultivated, just as fifty years earlier there had
been those who preferred the older rules of Lenôtre to
the new ones of Kent. What Peacock's Mr Milestone
really disapproved of was not a new set of rules but the
new tendency to abolish rules altogether, the new preference for natural scenic beauty over man-made beauty;
it was the tradition still persisting, that Nature herself
is crude and must be refined by man to be palatable.
At first sight this new attitude towards natural beauty
might seem to be symptomatic of what is always called
for convenience the "romantic movement", but it is
really less a symptom than a consequence, a comparatively late development, for when the earlier
"romantics", about the mid-eighteenth century, turned
their attention to Nature they generally noticed only
her idyllic qualities and were very strictly selective in
their admiration; after the, so to speak, publication of

72

selected aspects, the arbiters of taste perhaps unwisely introduced their public to the whole works of Nature at the moment when, for various reasons, they were beginning to lose their authority over that public; the result was an almost obligatory admiration of all natural scenery, unselective and uncritical, which has lasted till to-day. Nobody can really doubt the obligatory nature of this rite of admiration who has seen the crowds at any of the recognised beauty-spots of England or Switzerland on a fine day.

It is perhaps inaccurate to describe this admiration as unselective, for certain types of view always evoke more rapture than others, especially the spectacular or the extensive; obviously such views will evoke a stronger emotion than what is intimate or familiar, since the art of seeing is not very widely practised and only the striking can hope to attract attention; this is because during the last century only the more spectacular achievements of Nature have remained untouched by man, and man has become so conscious of his power that recognition of a power greater than his own reminds him automatically of God; the instinct that sends him to visit a beauty-spot is the same instinct that sends him to church, and he will arrange his thoughts and emotions at the one as conscientiously and as mechanically as in the other. It has long been the duty of a right-thinking Christian to regard God as his Father, but it has even longer been his instinct to regard Nature as his Mother; that instinct, however, became dormant in the nineteenth century when Nature appeared to be his servant, almost his slave, so entirely at his service that he regarded with some contempt those earlier generations who had been content to use only what Nature

73

chose to give them and no more; yet this contempt was tempered with indulgence, and indulgence implies affection, and even the progressive machine-making modern of the mid-nineteenth century contemplated the works of the past as a soothing contrast to his own bewilderingly rapid movement. The further he receded into the past the stronger grew that contrast, until out of what had been indulgent affection there developed an admiration, which in turn produced the ambition to imitate the Middle Ages, and that which had half captured the imagination of Romantic England wholly captured that of Industrial England; Antiquity and the Classic [1] disappeared together with the Renaissance, and the Gothic was regarded as the only fit model for the mid-nineteenth century to copy.

Many factors contributed to the making of the Gothic revival in the nineteenth century, and the movement had many prophets, most of whom believed that they really were reviving a style forgotten and neglected since the Renaissance; some of the leaders of the movement, however, did remember that the eighteenth century too had had a Gothic revival, but took care in remembering to cast discredit on what had been done by always describing it as "gimcrack", "pantomime" or "Strawberry Hill" Gothic; for Strawberry Hill and its creator Horace Walpole seemed to be the epitome of eighteenth-century Gothic tastes, and as such were mistrusted.

It is evident that during the greater part of the nineteenth century Horace Walpole was very gravely mis-

---

[1] Amongst the latest buildings in the classic taste were the British Museum by Smirke, 1847, and the Ashmolean Museum by Cockerell, 1841–5.

trusted, probably because he did not fulfil the obligations of his class in his day as the nineteenth century
liked to see them; the son of a Prime Minister, he took
no part in politics; an aristocrat, yet not a rake; com-
fortably rich, yet a writer of books; pretending to
learning, yet dangerously witty. It is a favourite English
contention, not peculiar to the nineteenth century,
that no man can excel in more than one activity, and
since it was conceded that Walpole excelled in the art
of letter-writing, it was held to be presumptuous that
he should attempt to excel elsewhere; admittedly, his
Anecdotes of Painting in England was freely drawn on by
writers on English art, but neither those writers nor
their readers were very numerous. Even so, the shortcomings of the *Anecdotes* have been continuously and
conscientiously pointed out by a succession of critics
and historians who forget that but for that work our
knowledge of painting in England down to about 1750
would be even smaller than it is. It is true that the chief
credit is due to George Vertue, who accumulated all
the notes and raw material, and it is probable that
Vertue would have done it better than did Walpole,
since he seems to have had a more accurate mind and a
greater energy in the pursuit of facts. But Vertue did
not live to carry out his intention, and Walpole was
sufficiently interested to buy the manuscripts[1] from his
widow and undertake the considerable task of selection and compilation. We are sometimes inclined to
forget that historical knowledge has greatly increased
in the last half-century and our critical faculty has therefore become more discriminating; any similar work of
that period, by whomever written, would seem to us

[1] Now being published *in extenso* by the Walpole Society.

75

inaccurate in many respects. The point is not that the work is done less well than it might have been, but that Horace Walpole took the trouble to do it. A further and even more convincing proof of his deep interest in the arts lies in the *Journals of Visits to Country Seats, 1751–1784*,[1] note-books filled with observations, ranging over more than thirty years, that suggest the professional scholar much more than the idle and flippant dilettante.

It has been the fate of the miniature Gothic castle known as Strawberry Hill to have been in the limelight almost continuously since Walpole first bought his "toy out of Mrs Chenevix's shop"[2] in 1747 and re-christened it Strawberry. It was not the first piece of Gothic in the eighteenth century, nor, very certainly, was it the last; it was not the biggest nor, perhaps, was it the best; but it was by far the most famous, possibly by reason of the large number of Walpole's friends, all of whom were kept informed as to the progress of the works; our knowledge of it is complete, not only because it still exists not greatly altered, but also by reason of the description with illustrations and complete catalogue of its contents issued by Walpole from his private press in 1784. It used to be regarded as a convenient starting-point for the Gothic revival, but since the recent renewal of interest in such architects as Vanbrugh and Hawksmoor we have become more familiar with what might, were it not so cumbrous an expression, be called pre-Walpole neo-Gothic. We can see a faint stream of traditional Gothic[3] flowing down

---

[1] Edited by Paget Toynbee. Walpole Society, vol. xvi., 1927–8.

[2] Walpole took over the lease from Mrs Chenevix, who kept a famous toy-shop or jeweller's *à la mode*, and restored its original name. The reconstruction began about 1750.

[3] See Kenneth Clarke, *The Gothic Revival*, 1928.

through the sixteenth and seventeenth centuries, partly by way of local traditions and partly in the occasional practice of the greater architects; but in spite of the more obvious examples, such as the Hall staircase of Christchurch in Oxford,[1] and the tracery of the great west window of Tewkesbury Abbey,[1] the Gothic manner is so thoroughly alien to the seventeenth and earlier eighteenth centuries that the attempt to establish continuity, though ingenious and interesting, only serves to show more clearly that these rare and scattered Gothicisms are due either to the necessity for the new building not to swear with the old, as are Wren's works at Westminster and Oxford,[2] or to an antiquarian interest on the part of the architect as are some of Hawksmoor's and Wren's[3] churches and the former's building at All Souls.

By the end of the reign of Anne an architectural tradition was established; but it was not the Gothic, for that was sneered away into the background of the dim and barbarous past; it was the tradition of Palladio and Vitruvius, Inigo Jones and Christopher Wren. The number of Gothic (or at least Gothistic) buildings put up in England before the reconstruction of Strawberry Hill is quite considerable; Oxford possesses most of the more hackneyed examples, such as parts of Christchurch, St. John's, University and All Souls. Hawksmoor, Gibbs and Vanbrugh all worked now and then in what they conceived to be the old manner; Batty Langley, laughed at in his own day and methodically beaten with the same stick ever since, had both the

[1] 1640 and 1686 respectively.

[2] *E.g.* Tom Tower.

[3] St. Michael's, Cornhill, and St. Dunstan's-in-the-East are probably Wren's best Gothic churches.

architect's appreciation of and the antiquarian's interest in the Gothic and was genuinely concerned to revive it, however much he may, in fact, have misunderstood it; Dugdale, Evelyn and Anthony à Wood, the stock seventeenth-century antiquarians, show that love of Gothic was not by any means dead; but these instances, which could still, no doubt, be multiplied, only emphasise the "museum" character of this very early neo-Gothic. To make a modern analogy, perhaps 150 years hence some student of the history of Taste will endeavour to establish the unbroken continuity of the Baroque from the reign of Charles II to that of George V, and out of the evidence provided by Mrs Esdaile and Mr Sacheverell Sitwell he will prove that that style, so much in favour in certain circles of the middle 1920's, was not a Baroque revival but a late flowering of a *seicento* tradition. But other students of the same subject may regard these critics as being merely special pleaders for a form of art so long dead as to be, on its revival, novel; while for every decade from 1750 to 1920 one could no doubt find a book, a pamphlet, an article, to show that at least one person remembered Vanbrugh or Bernini, yet ultimately Ruskin and the *Seven Lamps of Architecture* prove stronger than any argument produced by however well mustered an array of isolated prophets. And the effect of *Vitruvius Britannicus* on the eighteenth century is almost as great as that of the *Seven Lamps* on the nineteenth, for pagan Rome was as supreme in the one century as the Middle Ages were in the next, and in spite of carefully marshalled facts there remains something to be said in favour of the old-fashioned habit of describing the Gothic Revival as a *Revival*.

All the same, it is probable that, had there not been

a Horace Walpole, all the Batty Langleys in the world would have availed but little and that the revival would have had to wait for Beckford for its first effectual impetus; and Beckford's almost legendary activities occurred more than half a century after Walpole's. That is to imply that it might have had to wait for the romantic influence that by 1800 had already deeply affected politics, painting and literature and that it would not have begun, as actually it did, from intellectual rather than emotional motives. Walpole's interest in the Gothic is purely antiquarian, with sentiment playing only so large a part, as it always does when a scholar pursues his favourite subject; it is of course customary to dismiss Walpole's scholarship as negligible and incomplete, an attitude inevitable in an age of somewhat arid specialists; yet few eighteenth-century critics, with the exception of John Carter, were so pedantically insistent as Walpole on what he genuinely believed to be fidelity to the original models, and he would never have approved of such inconsistencies as occurred later in the century, as, for example, a room with Gothic panelling, Gothic bookshelves and Gothic doors and mantelpieces, yet with a barrel-shaped ceiling painted in the manner of Angelica Kauffmann.[1] That Walpole was a stickler for accuracy is shown in the following quotation,[2] descriptive of Cobham, in August 1761: "Went again to Mr Charles Hamilton's . . . to see the Gothic building and the Roman ruin. The former is taken from Batty Langley's book (which does not contain a single design of true or good Gothic) and is made

---

[1] *E.g.* at Arbury, in Warwickshire.
[2] *Horace Walpole's Journals of Visits to Country Seats, etc.* Walpole Society, vol. xvi.

worse by pendent ornaments in the arches, and by being closed in on two sides at bottom with cheeks that have no relation to Gothic. The whole is an unmeaning edifice. In all Gothic designs, they should be made to imitate something that was of that time, a part of a church, a castle, a convent or a mansion. The Goths never built summer-houses or temples in a garden. This at Mr Hamilton's stands on the brow of a hill— there an imitation of a fort or watch-tower had been proper. The Ruin is much better imagined, but has great faults. It represents a triumphal Arch, and yet could never have had a column, which would certainly have accompanied so rich a soffit. Then this Arch is made to have been a Columbarium. You may as well suppose an Alderman's family buried *in* Temple Bar." Walpole was always looking out for Gothic in all his tours and visits; very few examples escaped his notice, and many were adversely criticised as, for example, what he saw at Burleigh in July 1763: "Brown is ornamenting the Park and has built a Gothic greenhouse and stables, which are not bad, except that they do not accord with the house, which is not Gothic". But praise also he distributes, as at Wentworth Castle, in September 1768: "Ruins of a large imaginary City on an opposite hill, well-placed. A Gothic arch under a Wood, Do., a Gothic farm, Do. Nobody has a better taste than this Lord." [1] It is this very seriousness of mid-eighteenth-century Gothic building that produces a conscious and deliberate artificiality almost more attractive than the unwitting artificiality of the early nineteenth; this mid-eighteenth-century interest in the Gothic springs directly from the antiquarianism

[1] Lord Strafford.

that was so rapidly becoming the fashion, while by the later part of the same century and the beginning of the next the style had acquired an associational interest, which, while giving it a greater degree of self-consciousness, at the same time blinded its devotees to its real nature. These regarded their new parish churches and their country-houses as the direct descendants, in unbroken continuity, of the medieval cathedrals and castles, while their grandparents had never lost sight of the fact that they were imitating and reconstructing or, in fact, adapting.

Not that every squire or wealthy nabob who Gothicised his country-seat during the 1750's or 1760's was a medieval scholar; but there was certainly, after about 1740, a widespread interest among educated people in archaeology, and an interest in the past became a fashionable affectation; it is possible that this was helped by the large number of hitherto obscure persons ennobled by Sir Robert Walpole or, a little later, by the Duke of Newcastle, both of whom were admirable party-managers, and both of whom found it convenient to ensure the support of as many as possible of the new and immense fortunes being brought home from India or the further East; the offer of a peerage was seldom refused, and the College of Heralds was busily employed in the finding of suitable pedigrees; and many of these newer recruits to the privileged classes were anxious to make the houses on their recently bought estates look more nearly as if they had been built by the founder of their line. Gothicistic detail and ornament inside, battlements and pinnacles outside were already increasingly in demand before Horace Walpole built a completely Gothic house; then the fashion was confirmed, as a fashion.[1] As interest in the Middle Ages increased, connoisseurship also increased, and since the eighteenth century was always careful to study its emotions in relation to any given scene or experience, it was soon realised that in order to complete the effect of a newly Gothicised house mere architecture was not enough; care must be taken to reproduce the air of gloom and darkness associated since the beginning of the revival with Gothic: an idea proceeding partly from the overgrown and more or less ruinous condition of such survivals as were left, partly from the knowledge that in an age when glass was not in common use windows must necessarily have been small and inadequate. To conjure up the past is always a solemn undertaking, associated with mystery and a sense of the transitoriness of mortal things, and very soon such symbols of the Gothic past as church towers, ivy, owls, monks, hermits and Crusaders began to assume an importance greater than that of the civilisation they were supposed to represent. The revival had, in fact, reached its second stage by the beginning of the last quarter of the century and had already begun to be weighed down by its burden of associations.

Ideas political, sociological or philosophical were all at one time or another associated with the Gothic idiom; it is traceable in every aspect of the Romantic movement soon to sweep Europe, of which the French Revolution was one of the most logical results; what could be more romantic than the idea of men living in an arcadian condition of social equality? Marie-Antoinette had played at it in her toy farm, while Mrs Graham

---

[1] Eastlake, *Gothic Revival*, cap. 5, gives a list of houses newly built in the Gothic manner, or old houses Gothicised, after 1800.

permitted herself to be painted as a housemaid and the Duchess of Queensberry sat to Hudson as a country girl. Shepherds and shepherdesses are not Gothic, but they are romantic and the Gothic at this stage was a symptom of romanticism. The millionaire Beckford took it to its next stage, and made it dramatic; so dramatic, or melodramatic, that it soon became necessary to revise all the old ideas about the Gothic, and put it on a sounder basis; otherwise, like the tower of his house at Fonthill, it would have collapsed in a heap of rubbish. But perhaps it would be exaggeration to say that Beckford influenced the romantic movement, for he was but a product of it; he was a dramatist who lived his life and built his dwelling-places in terms of the theatre; he was an actor who played the leading rôle in his own dramas, a producer who designed his own scenery and set the stage himself. The eighteenth- or nineteenth-century Englishman was emphatically not a man of the theatre, and was not likely to be permanently affected, or even much impressed, by the theatrical.[1] Men marvelled at Fonthill but did not imitate it; they stared at it, invented wild tales of what went on inside it, and, when it fell down, forgot it. That was barely a century ago and already it is no more than a legend; we have many contemporary accounts of it,[2] but only Turner can illumine

[1] There are two notable exceptions to this generalisation; unquestionably the statesman who most completely captured the imagination of his age was Chatham, yet Chatham's histrionic powers were hardly inferior to Garrick's. And Nelson was to his contemporaries, and has been ever since, greater and more vital than St. Vincent, Howe or Bridport because he had sufficient imagination to take the methods of the theatre with him on to the quarter-deck. What else is the significance of the telescope at Copenhagen or the signal at Trafalgar?

[2] The best are: J. Rutter, *Delineations of Fonthill*, 1823; J. Storer, *A Description of Fonthill Abbey*, 1812; J. Britton, *Illustrations of Fonthill Abbey, etc.*, 1823.

for us the mind of Beckford and show us how it was intended to appear (which, in justice to its cloud-climbing owner, is probably exactly how it did appear); in these water-colours we see the great tower piercing the thunderstorms, or, in rivalry to the neighbouring Salisbury, darting in sunlight up from the fat downs. Like Ely or Gloucester it was a focal-point for all the surrounding country; since, however, Fonthill was not a cathedral but a house it was inevitable that it should be pronounced eccentric and looked on, if not with amazement, certainly with suspicion, just as Beckford must have appeared suspicious to his neighbours; a man who, inheriting a fine mansion, should pull down that mansion and build another and a greater, might be thought extravagant; but when he proceeded to pull that down in turn and replace it by yet another, even larger and with, moreover, a soaring tower, employing two armies of workmen labouring alternately by day and night (the tower collapsed immediately it was completed, and was promptly put up again), then beyond doubt he must be thought eccentric; finally, for a man so wealthy and so evidently original[1] to live alone in celibate aloofness was in the highest degree suspicious. Even those most susceptible to the allure of abbeys felt that Fonthill was sinister; probably there was considerable relief when Beckford sold the place,[2] and went away to Bath, where he built himself another tower.[3]

[1] He inherited £100,000 a year, and wrote *Vathek* in French at a single sitting of three days and two nights.

[2] He sold it in 1822 for £330,000, having completed it by 1807. The tower collapsed for the second time soon after the sale and the place was dismantled. The tower had no foundations, owing to the fraudulence of the contractor, who on his death-bed had expressed contrition and at the same time surprise that it should have stood so long.

[3] Lansdowne Tower.

Strawberry Hill and Fonthill

None of the motives usually found behind eighteenth-century Gothic are present in the building of Fonthill; Beckford was no Langley or Walpole, anxious for accuracy and precision; he was no Wyatt, adapting the ecclesiastical to the domestic. Fonthill certainly was romantic enough, but its idiom was unfamiliar since it is impossible to "associate" it with anything except a cathedral (not really even an abbey, that would have been easier), and a cathedral quite clearly it was not; since it was unsuitable to feel about a private house the emotion proper about cathedrals, and since the only other emotion possible, astonishment, was equally unfitted to a private house, the only course to adopt was condemnation; and condemned it was, to sterility. Fonthill gave birth to nothing and, though its name continued, its features passed out of mind. The memory of the great building must always be as of something apart from the main stream of the Gothic movement, an unexpected piece of treasure-trove carried in on the tide of romanticism and crumbling as it struck the shore.

It is perhaps inapt to compare the Gothic fashion to the flowing of a tide, since the spectacle of two distinct tides flowing simultaneously is rarely seen; while two distinct fashions, each in turn divided into two or more, are seen continually throughout the eighty years from 1750 to 1830, the Gothic and the Classical; the former can be, in addition to the medieval, either Chinese, Rustic or Picturesque, while the latter can be Greek, Roman, Egyptian or Renaissance; moreover, any of these divisions or sub-divisions can be used for any purpose. At the end of the 1767 edition of Batty Langley's *Builder's Director* are some very illuminating bookseller's advertisements, which are worth quoting

85

at length. The first is "Abbott's Grand, Magnificent and Superb Designs for Coaches and Chariots; the Pannels are finely enriched with Landscapes, genteel Sweeps, Festoons, Ornaments for the Arms, Supporters, Crests, Coronets, Cyphers, etc." This rococo repertoire cost 10s. 6d. Then we have "The Temple Builder's most useful Companion, being Fifty entire new original Designs for Pleasure and Recreation; consisting of Plans, Elevations and Sections in the Greek, Roman and Gothic Taste; calculated for the ornamenting of Parks, Forests, Woods, Gardens, Canals, Eminences, extensive Views, Mounts, Vistas, Islands, etc." Finally "Grotesque Architecture or Rural Amusement; consisting of Plans, Elevations and Sections, for Huts, Summer and Winter Hermitages, Retreats, Terminaries, Chinese, Gothic and natural Grottos, Cascades, Rustic Seats, Baths, Mosques, Moresque Pavillions, Grotesque Seats, Green-Houses etc., many of which may be executed with Flints, Irregular Stones, Rude Branches and Roots of Trees". All this could be bought for 4s. 6d., and one is pleased to think that those who employed hermits considered the comfort of their human "local-colour" to the extent of giving them suitable accommodation for all seasons. Almost all the important architects of the period worked in first one and then another of the prevailing styles; Sir William Chambers, for example, uses first the Chinese and then the Classic; Wyatt begins as a Classic builder and then adopts the Gothic; Nash, mainly Classic, can yet use the Oriental with great skill; only the Adam brothers are not various, and cling consistently to their debasement of the Palladian.[1]

1 Their few Gothistic experiments are very timid.

Strawberry Hill and Fonthill

In view of the obviously ecclesiastical flavour of the Gothic, it is strange that while later eighteenth-century mansions were quite as often crocheted and pinnacled as not, yet the churches built during that same period were almost always neo-Roman and, later, neo-Greek; neither Renaissance, nor Baroque, nor even Adam, but a form of "neo-Parthenon" with a spire added above the pediment. Certainly, remarkably few churches of any kind were being built under George III, due probably to the fact that those whose private enterprise might in another age have built churches and endowed them were at this time apathetic towards religion, and those who were not apathetic were generally dissenters, "enthusiasts". In time, however, ecclesiastical fervour returned and the Greco-Roman temples scattered about London began to seem very inapt, even quite unchristian: considerable stir was caused by this discovery, but though it was thought most unsuitable that Christian churches should be adapted from Greek models, it was not thought incongruous to build private houses in a style adapted from medieval churches. The final victory of the Gothic may be said to have arrived with the building of such landmarks as St. Luke's Church, Chelsea,[1] and the New Court of St. John's College, Cambridge.[2]

By that time the new Gothic had moved far from its archaeological beginning, having become first romantic and then almost entirely associational (which is an inevitable development from the generally "romantic" phase); but precisians still raised their voices in protest

[1] 1819–24.

[2] 1825–31; built, together with the "Bridge of Sighs", by Rickman and John Hutchinson. Hutchinson was responsible for the bridge itself. See *Country Life*, 15th November 1930.

against "false" Gothic building and against ignorant or injudicious restorations or repairs. John Carter is by far the most vigorous and the most vigilant of such; his career begins in the 1780's and 1790's with various volumes of "Antiquities", but from 1798 till his death in 1817 there is an almost ceaseless stream of protesting letters from his indignant pen; from indignation he moves to frenzy, from frenzy to despair. Himself moving spiritually in the Middle Ages,[1] he could not bear to see the Gothic so misused; for to such as Carter it was in most cases misuse, as comparatively few architects made any study of the medieval; James Essex was perhaps the first professional architect to do so, and his drawings of the wall-paintings in Eton College chapel[2] showed that he had a love as well as a knowledge of the subject still in his day rather rare. Essex was employed at Strawberry by Horace Walpole from 1773, after he had paid off William Robinson, who had been carrying out Bentley's designs there since the beginning. Towards the end of the century, however, in spite of the example of Walpole and the protests of Carter, architects were openly proclaiming that they aimed at the spirit of Gothic rather than at the exact forms; about 1800 James Wyatt began the Gothicising of Charles II's State apartments in Windsor Castle, and began thereby the process which resulted in the Windsor we know to-day:[3] during the eighteenth century the Castle had been badly neglected and had become

---

[1] He appears to have written two operas, *The White Rose* and *The Cell of St. Oswald*; they deal with English life in the Middle Ages. The scores and libretti are both his own, and he also painted the scenery. See Eastlake, *The Gothic Revival*.

[2] Walpole Society, vol. xvii.

[3] See W. H. St. John Hope, *Architectural History of Windsor Castle*, 1913.

quite inadequate as a residence, so that George III and Queen Charlotte had to find outside accommodation for the greater part of their family and Court. It was not until the accession of George IV that the Castle was really made habitable, and transformed from a rambling, half-ruined cluster into a complete and dignified whole. If the outside of the building now contains little more of the original fabric than does the outside of Westminster Abbey, there is nothing to regret in that; it stands to-day as a monument to the taste and dramatic genius of the King and his architect, Sir Jeffrey Wyatville.[1] Carlton House vanished a century ago, the Pavilion at Brighton still bravely continues to exist, unoccupied and very carefully preserved, like a mandarin's robe in a museum, but Windsor is more alive and far more impressive than it can ever have been before; the Round Tower was nearly doubled in height by Wyatville, which gives at once the necessary emphasis to an outline that would otherwise have been rather uneventful, and when, in addition to the outside improvements, Sir Thomas Lawrence had contributed his share to the embellishment of the inside, then at last George had a Castle fit for even the First Gentleman to inhabit.

Windsor, however, can without exaggeration be termed exceptional, just as can its royal restorer; architects other than Wyatville had to work for patrons less exalted and without the King's financial advantage; since the process of Gothicising implied the substitution of stone for brick, and since there was not

[1] Originally Jeffrey Wyatt, nephew of James Wyatt; his name and his arms were honourably augmented by George IV when laying the foundation stone of the new works.

always a quarry conveniently near, it naturally follows that very soon there was a demand for some material cheaper and more practicable than the real thing, and the age of Stucco thereupon began. Almost all the difference between the Gothic revival under Walpole and Bentley and the next stages of the movement under Wyatt and Pugin is this same difference between stone and stucco. It means a decline in honesty, or at least a change in aesthetic standards. The earlier revivalists tried so far as they were able to imitate given models in the appropriate materials, while their successors were content to reproduce the general appearance and create the necessary effect in a method economically sounder. It was obviously easier and cheaper to cover brickwork with plaster or stucco than to pull it down and replace it with stone.

After many mistakes and the consequent uncomfortable shocks we to-day have begun to learn a little wisdom; we no longer assume that our own age is necessarily the most enlightened that the world has yet seen. We are learning a little humility, and have realised the arrogance of condemning any taste that disagrees with our own; or perhaps it is not wisdom, nor humility, but only extreme caution. Whatever it may be, we are at least prepared to find something pleasing in everything our fathers and grandfathers thought displeasing, and have rejected fixed and rigid canons that we may set ourselves at liberty to change our minds and our views every year; if we acquire no standards, we at least acquire a little knowledge. With the knowledge, and despite the toleration that is born of it, there has come also a more general and a sharper critical appreciation of the arts, and of, more especially, architecture. It may be objected that the existence of criticism implies standards; but these now are no longer the single-point-of-view standards of a few generations ago; a work of art, whether it be an etching or a general post office, in any taste or style is accepted provided it is faithful to the principles of that taste and, in the case of architecture, is faithful also to the requirements postulated by the purpose for which it was built. We can still admire an Elizabethan manor-house, but we do not admire that same style when it is used for a large shop in the middle of a modern city. That is to suggest that at last we are learning to mistrust shams, and moreover to recognise them when we see them. The architect[1] of to-day is guilty less often than at any time in the last 130 years of trying to imitate an effect which is in the given circumstances superfluous or of using one material to imitate the character or texture of another. A steel-skeleton block of offices or flats no longer invariably tries to look as if it were built of stone or brick throughout; while up to a few years ago massive stone pilasters were stuck on to the front of buildings to support no weight whatever, we now occasionally see ferro-concrete content to look like ferro-concrete. This seems to indicate an encouraging return of honesty, and also of intelligence.

England, however, in the beginning of the nineteenth century was becoming commercially so prosperous that there was not much time for honesty, and politically so democratic that there was not much demand for intelligence. A great many buildings for all purposes were being put up, country-houses, townhouses, shops, whole new residential or commercial

---

1 Not to be confused with the speculative builder.

streets, churches, banks, theatres and public-houses; sometimes they were in the Gothic manner and sometimes, so long at least as the influences of the French Revolution and the First Empire were keenly felt, in the Classic manner. Most architects were able to use both, and since in both an appearance of stone was necessary stucco was the almost universal medium; apart from the aesthetic aspect of Regency Gothic or Greek, stucco columns or stucco pinnacles do seem to argue a decline in perception and sensibility from the level of the 1750's, not because there was more sham, but because the shams either were not realised or were thought to be as good as what they were supposed to imitate.

CHAPTER VI

COLLECTORS AND CRITICS

THE last chapter was much concerned with Horace
Walpole, who, whether abused or praised, is very
generally regarded as one of the leading figures in the
history of the arts in England, for it is impossible to
omit the part he played, whether it be regarded as that
of hero, villain or comic relief. But the part played by
his father Sir Robert Walpole in the same comedy tends
to be overlooked, sometimes ignored altogether; yet if
the works of art he brought together were still together,
and in England, he would be regarded as a prince of
collectors and his memory be kept alive by something
more tangible than fiscal reforms or a foreign policy;
but his collection was sold by his grandson and the
major part bought by Catherine the Great to ornament
her upstart, pseudo-European capital, and the memory
of it in this country soon faded.

Consequently it has been the fashion among historians
to show Sir Robert Walpole, though eminently distinguished as a statesman, to be of a coarse and earthy
quality as a man, and, when confronted with the fact
of the picture-gallery at Houghton, to say that it is
the instinct of all new, self-made millionaires to buy
pictures by established Old Masters in order to acquire
a dignity they have not inherited; the Walpoles were
certainly conscious of the newness of their wealth and
nobility, though Horace turns it skilfully to advantage:

93

"Could those virtuous men, your Father and Grand-father, arise from yonder church, how would they be amazed to see this noble edifice and spacious plantation, where once stood their plain homely dwelling!"[1] The son's admiration and affection for his father impelled him to the description of Houghton and its contents in which occurs the above-quoted passage; but in the same work occurs the following: "Commerce, which carries along with it the Curiosities and Arts of Countries, as well as the Riches, daily brings us something from Italy. How many valuable Collections of Pictures are there established in England on the frequent ruins and dispersion of the finest Galleries in Rome and other Cities!"; this, as a matter of fact, is not strictly accurate, for in the 1740's great collections were still rather the exception than the rule.

Before the Civil Wars, collecting had begun to be the vogue. King James I had not been without an interest in the arts,[2] though not perhaps very zealous; but the Earl of Arundel and the Duke of Buckingham, the Earl of Pembroke and Sir Balthasar Gerbier, Henry Prince of Wales and his brother Charles I, to say nothing of Rubens and Vandyck, sent their buyers and agents over all Europe, to report which Prince was prepared to part with the gem of his cabinet; the rivalry between them, intense as it was, occasionally was appeased by exchange or even by a gift, for Charles, of course, acquired several of his choicest pieces as presents from fellow-monarchs or their ambassadors. That Bucking-

---

[1] Horace Walpole, *Collected Works*: Dedication of *Aedes Walpolianae*, 1747, to his father, Sir Robert Walpole, 1st Earl of Orford.

[2] He first caused Vandyck to come to England, in 1620–21, though the experiment was successful on neither side.

ham was an ardent collector, and a serious rival to Arundel, is shown by his purchase of the Rubens Collection for £10,000 in 1627, though he did not live to enjoy his new possessions for long, as he was assassinated in the following year. Though the activities of Arundel, as a collector of antiquities as well as paintings, are part of history, Pembroke's activities are almost as important, for they were at least sufficient to cause Arundel the greatest anxiety when he contemplated this second rival's competition. Further, James I's son Henry, Prince of Wales, possessed an acquisitive love of beautiful things which caused him to be recognised throughout Europe before his death at the age of eighteen as an important collector; and his collection formed the nucleus of his brother's, Charles I's, perhaps the greatest ever brought together by one man in this country. Charles, in buying his Raphaels and Mantegnas, his Correggio and his Andrea del Sarto, was following a taste that was already general; but the catholicity of his individual taste is shown by his acquisition of the "Wilton" Diptych and his courageous patronage of such difficult moderns as Rembrandt. After the Civil Wars, however, collecting ceased to be fashionable, and did not become so again for a hundred years; though Lely, certainly, by his acquisitions of Old Master drawings, shows himself a collector as shrewd and critical as Rubens before him or Reynolds and Lawrence after him.

So when Walpole built Houghton and decided to fill it with pictures, he certainly was following no recent precedent, nor was his example followed very generally; his only formidable rival was the Duke of Marlborough, who also had a new dignity to support and a new palace to fill, and who also has suffered from the accusations of "millionairishness" brought against Walpole. When compared with their successors of a generation later, the Great of the time of Queen Anne or George I cannot with truth be described as instinctive collectors; and they were certainly not patrons, where the painters other than portraitists are concerned, though neither the architects nor the poets had cause to complain. Patrons, in fact, the English have seldom been; the nearest approach that we have made to such figures as Leo X, Lorenzo the Magnificent, Charles V or Francis I have been, perhaps, Henry VIII and George IV; Henry's patronage was not very extensive, while George IV was at least as much a collector as a patron. The distinction is important, since the collector never directly affects the arts but is concerned only with buying something for the production of which he has been in no way responsible, even if he buys the work of his own contemporaries (which, until the nineteenth century, Englishmen rarely did); the great patron, by providing a suitable material *milieu* enables and inspires the artist to create and can be said therefore to have a hand in such creation; lacking in himself the actual creative faculty, he can in part make good the deficiency by establishing this relationship between himself and those who, themselves productive, yet lack either the incentive or the opportunity to produce. Such a relationship is rarely found in this country, yet, until recent times, no other people have shown themselves so eager to be surrounded with pictures or willing to pay so heavily for the privilege; in 1765 a visiting Frenchman wrote home from London "a taste for pictures makes an article of their luxury; they sacrifice to this taste in proportion to their fortune".[1] It was well known among the dealers, and also among the private owners, of the Continent that the Englishman was willing to pay big prices for whatever took his fancy, and also that his critical knowledge was generally less than his enthusiasm, so that many of the canvases triumphantly hung up in the great houses masqueraded (and often still do so) under some august name to which their right was, at least, questionable. The money, of course, was spent on those Masters who had acquired immortality by being dead, and contemporary artists, especially Hogarth, were enraged that the fashionable man of taste should admire and value pictures solely in accordance with their antiquity, to the neglect of living painters. Hogarth showed his resentment in the famous tail-piece to the 1761 Exhibition of the Society of Artists, wherein the Ape, dressed as the Fop, assiduously waters three dead plants.

Criticism was suffering, as were the other and creative arts, from the rules drawn up and imposed by the Augustans; in vain the painters protested against the excessive attention paid by the collector to the critics; Reynolds wrote in 1759:[2] "But there is another kind of Critick (*i.e.* in addition to him who, unable to comprehend the whole, judges only by the parts) still worse, who judges by narrow rules, and those too often false, and which though they should be true and founded on nature will lead him but a very little way towards the just estimation of the sublime beauties in works of Genius." And later on, in the same letter (and it is necessary to remind oneself that this was written in

---

[1] Whitley, *Artists and their Friends in England*, i. 210.
[2] Letter to *The Idler*, 29th September 1759.

1759), he says: "Criticks, so far as I have observed, debar themselves from receiving any pleasure from the polite arts at the same time that they profess to love and admire them: for these rules being always uppermost, give them a propensity to criticize that, instead of giving up the reins of their imagination into their author's hands, their frigid minds are employed in examining whether the performance be according to the rules of art. . . ." But nobody listened to the painters; there were, after all, very many of them, and only a few were anything but second-rate; most of them, moreover, were poverty-stricken and had never travelled, or if they had were prejudiced or jealous.

The social position of artists, until after the middle of the century, was not exalted; of professional artists, that is to say, for it was rapidly becoming important for the Great to profess an interest in at least one of the arts. The professional artist, if attached to or protected by a nobleman, was a servant or a tradesman. It would probably have been better for him had he never tried to acquire social status, for thereby he gained but little and lost a measure of his independence; by entering the higher social world he became inevitably subject to the prejudices and snobberies of that world; though there must have been every inducement to escape from the position suggested in a letter written in 1743 by Lady Charlotte Fermor to her mother, Lady Pomfret:[1] "After supper we all danced to our own singing in order to teach Signor Casali (an Italian they have in the house) English country-dances; he is a painter, and I fancy as low-born as they generally are, though by means of an Order he wears, set in diamonds (which he

[1] Quoted by Whitley, *Artists and their Friends in England,* i. 120-21.

tells me was given him by the King of Prussia and which very few people can have), and some fine suits of clothes, he passes for the most complete fine gentleman in the world, and is treated upon an equal footing with the rest of the company. . . ." Lady Charlotte must have been staying in a rather unusual house, where a painter could be treated upon an equal footing with the rest of the company; but then, perhaps, that was because he was an Italian and courtesy demanded special treatment for a foreigner.

It is true that most eighteenth-century collectors spent their money either on the dead Masters or on the living artists of foreign schools; but there is another aspect of the question. The majority of those who complained of neglect were themselves artists, which possibly makes their attitude a little suspect. The portrait-painters never lacked support, and there is no doubt that portraiture was infinitely the best expression of the native talent: had the other branches of painting been of an equal excellence, probably they too would have been supported, but pure landscape of any school was not greatly in demand; religious painting cannot be produced in a Protestant country, and historical or mythological painting has seldom been well done in England. There seems to be no valid reason why anyone should support something ill-done merely because it is a native product. If Richard Wilson or Gainsborough (in his capacity as a painter of landscape) were neglected, it was not because they were English rather than foreign, or living rather than dead, but because their work was not suited to the prevailing taste; to condemn, therefore, those who failed to support them is dangerously like condemning them for bad taste. The often-quoted arguments, that artists have to live and that rich men ought to support home industries, is hardly relevant, since there is obviously a limited demand for works of art of any kind, and, since the majority of painters in any age are ill-suited to be painters, there are always far too many pictures being produced. If a painter is not supported by the public, he is hardly entitled to accuse the public of blindness, stupidity or malice; and if he sneers at the public for knowing nothing about art (in which he is probably right), he ought to realise that he is directing his work to the attention of a few on whose support alone he cannot, in any case, expect to live. The eighteenth-century collector, like his descendant of to-day, was not a philanthropist; at his worst he was a speculator; most often he was a follower of fashion; and at his best he was a cultivated person who paid to satisfy his own personal tastes and predilections; if, as occasionally happened, the work of a living native artist pleased him he bought it, and if not he left it alone. Even in the eighteenth century, merit in an artist was as rare as courage in a collector, but the one quality, when it occurred, was generally recognised and supported by the other.

One of the very few professional artists not dissatisfied with the condition of artists in England was Jonathan Richardson. "When Vandyke came hither, he brought face-painting to us; ever since which time (that is, for above fourscore years) England has excelled all the world in that great branch of the art; and being well stored with the works of the greatest masters, whether paintings or drawings, as well as the greatest encouragement, this may justly be esteemed as a complete and the best school for face-painting now in the world."[1] Nevertheless, not the most ardent supporter of his country's art could be expected to fill his house exclusively with paintings of faces; he, therefore, who wished for something further, was compelled to go abroad for it, to Italy or Flanders, and generally to Italy. Both the descriptions of collections and published expressions of opinion show clearly in what direction lay the preferences of collectors. The *Aedes Walpolianae*, a catalogue compiled by Horace Walpole of the collection formed at Houghton by his father, is a very good guide to what was held as Good Taste in the reigns of George I and George II; and the author's introductory criticisms add an individual note absent from most catalogues; in fact, to compare the *Aedes Walpolianae* with the *Description of Strawberry Hill* is to see not only the difference between the tastes of the father and of the son, but also that between the young and the middle-aged Horace Walpole. Sir Robert, in forming his great collection, was no doubt guided by those rules suggested by the connoisseurs, confirmed and strengthened by the dealers and accepted by the other millionaires. But Horace had an independence of taste which must have made him rejoice that he was not going to inherit Houghton and would therefore be able to form a collection of his own; the individuality of Strawberry is foreshadowed by certain remarks in the Introduction to the *Aedes*, such as the description of Andrea del Sarto's colouring as "a mixture of mist and tawdry", or the dismissal of the Dutch painters (always so popular in this country) as "those drudging Mimicks of Nature's most uncomely coarseness". He had this, however, in common with the rest of his age, that he places the

---

[1] Jonathan Richardson, *The Art of Painting*.

Roman School first, though he can criticise even them for too close a study of the Antique, the Venetian School second and the Florentine School nowhere; for him, as for almost all his contemporaries, the Milanese School exists solely by virtue of Leonardo, the Lombard by Correggio and Parmigiano, the Neapolitan by Salvator Rosa, the Flemish by Rubens; but he is, on the other hand, a little unusual in his praise of Lo Spagnoletto and of "Velasco", and in his preference of Le Sueur above Poussin, placing him in fact, for his great Ideas, second to Raphael. Finally, recapitulating his earlier remarks, and having criticised Correggio, Titian, Parmigiano and Poussin, he ends with: "In short, in my opinion, all the qualities of a perfect Painter never met but in Raphael, Guido and Annibal Carracci". Walpole was thirty when he wrote that; anybody else of his generation rash enough (and almost everyone was rash enough) to name three perfect painters would certainly have retained Raphael but would probably have substituted Michelangelo for one of the others.

Thirty or forty years later official taste is clearly laid down by Sir Joshua Reynolds in the "Discourses".[1] An analysis of these shows that Raphael and Michelangelo are mentioned in very nearly every Discourse. Although the Fifteenth is almost devoted to the latter, and ends with a panegyric on him, Raphael is constantly referred to as "The Divine", "him whom our enthusiasm honours with the name of Divine", "the first of painters", and so on; it is understood that the masters most to be

[1] The fifteen Discourses were pronounced at the Royal Academy School prize-givings; the first ten were published in 1778, and the authoritative edition of the fifteen by Malone in 1797.

esteemed after these two are the Carracci, Guido, Rosa, Poussin, Lorrain, Parmigiano, Titian, Tintoret and Correggio. All forms of painting, and all schools, are passed under the microscope of Sir Joshua's scholarly mind. Sculpture and even architecture are considered; he has a fine appreciation of Vanbrugh in the Thirteenth Discourse, though Bernini is condemned in the Tenth, while on the subject of antique sculpture he praises highly the Laocoon and prefers the grace and animated negligence of "the Apollo" (*sic*) to the "vulgar eagerness" of the Discobolus. The earlier schools, naturally, are almost ignored, Mantegna, Perugino and Dürer being grouped together as "old painters", while Masaccio is, in the Thirteenth Discourse, made the starting-point for a general criticism of the early Italians, and the early Flemings and Germans, such as Dürer and Lucas van Leyden, are given a little much-qualified praise in the Sixth. Vandyck is held by Sir Joshua to be, on the whole, the first of portrait-painters and "Frank Halls" is compared with him most unfavourably; as to the French, very little mention is made of any besides Poussin, Claude Lorrain and Le Sueur, though Rigaud is admitted to have merit, entirely overpowered, however, by "a total absence of simplicity", and Boucher, though he too is not without merit, has bad taste and his imitators are "abominable"; this, in the Thirteenth Discourse, is the only occasion on which the President in his official capacity permits himself to use such a word.

While the Discourses were thus intended as the Official Guide to the study of painting for Academy Students, the *Letters* of Reynolds, though few and mostly short, generally confirm the views embodied in the

Discourses; he rarely discusses painters when writing to his friends, but in 1769[1] he writes to James Barry that "the Cappella Sistina is the production of the greatest genius that was ever employed in the arts", and in 1776 to Giuseppe Pelli "il merito altissimo del divino vostro Michelangelo, sempre offrendolo non solo come principale, ma come unico modello a tutti coloro che in essa coltivano l'arti del Disegno". In 1785 he tells the Duke of Rutland that "Poussin certainly ranks amongst the first of the first rank of painters"; the Duke respected Sir Joshua's knowledge of the market, as is evident from this letter of 1785; he contemplated buying Poussin's set of the Seven Sacraments and, asking Sir Joshua's advice, was assured by him that the suggested price of £2000 for the set was very cheap; the following year Sir Joshua tells him that he holds Velasquez' portrait of Leo X to be "one of the first portraits in the world". Other letters to the Duke of Rutland show Sir Joshua's activities, not only as a collector, but, in a smaller way, as a dealer; he attends a sale in Brussels in 1785, at which he buys five Rubens, three Vandycks and a Snyders; in 1787 he sells the Duke a Dürer portrait, which he describes as "a rare and curious thing", and in a letter of 1786 he describes to him a Bernini group, about 8 feet high, which has cost him 700 guineas and which he hopes to be able to sell for a thousand.

In connection with the famous Fourteenth Discourse a letter to Lord Ossory in 1786 is particularly interesting; in discussing the exchange of something in his collection for what he believes to be a Titian, he says:

[1] These quotations are taken from the *The Letters of Sir Joshua Reynolds*, ed. by Frederick Whiley Hilles, 1929.

"What if I gave Gainsborough's Pigs[1] for it, it is by far the best Picture he ever painted or perhaps ever will"; Sir Joshua evidently wanted the Titian very badly, so that this letter should perhaps not be taken too seriously as his implied opinion of Gainsborough's portraiture. While his views on other painters are expressed clearly and not infrequently, his expressed views on his own work are rare enough to justify the quotation of a letter written in March 1782 to James Beattie: "I am much obliged to you for the honourable place you have given me cheek by jowl with Raphael and Titian, but I seriously think these names are too great to be associated with any modern name whatever; even if that modern was equal to either of them it would oppose too strongly our prejudices. I am far from wishing to decline the honour of having my name inserted, but I should think it will do better by itself . . . and in the second place where I am mentioned, leaving out Titian, I shall make a respectable figure." Sir Joshua's treatment of his less discriminating admirers was considerably more humane than that of Dr. Johnson, who generally expended his heaviest artillery on those who were least invulnerable.

If, during most of the eighteenth century, the dictates of the Augustans were obeyed by the orthodox from Reynolds downwards, a change began to be visible at the beginning of the nineteenth; the supremacy of the Ancients in sculpture certainly remained unquestioned, but both the Apelles legend and the perfection of the High Renaissance were accepted a little less readily. The modern English were beginning to be recognised apart from portrait-painting (in France as

[1] Now in the Collection at Castle Howard.

well as in England); and the seventeenth-century Dutchmen were beginning their long spell of popularity, in fact, they were becoming so popular that Wilkie was held in favour almost entirely by reason of his supposed resemblance to Jan Steen, and when he departed from that he was severely reproved, as happened in the case of his "Blind Man's Buff", exhibited in the Academy exhibition of 1813. "This excellent artist", said one of the reviews, "is declining into a prettyism similar to Watteau. He should shake off this feebleness."[1] Not only had the "drudging mimicks" come into their own, but the very unclassical landscapes of Gainsborough were as much in favour as the polite domesticities of Wheatley and the pig-sties of the drunken Morland; and despite the championship of Sir George Beaumont, the supremacy of Claude was seriously challenged by the belated admiration for Richard Wilson. Hazlitt, independent and almost alone as usual, denied that Wilson was superior to Claude, for though he admired Wilson's colour and chiaroscuro, he thought him deficient in workmanship and technical skill; he is unusually courageous in expressing also his strong dislike of Gainsborough's excessive slightness and slenderness; he was able to see that, just as many of his portraits approximate to the quality of clumsy pastels, so many of his landscapes are like bad water-colours; he described these as flimsy caricatures of Rubens.

However, this is digressing into the future. The fact remains that when collecting became a fashionable pursuit about the middle of the eighteenth century the great majority of those who bought pictures did so in obedience to the commands of authority, deaf to

---

[1] Quoted by Whitley, *Art in England, 1800–1820*.

the vituperation of Hogarth. First Italy, then the Low Countries, were ransacked by the collectors and the dealers; France, too, was thoroughly searched, though hardly for the work of her native painters, for very few collections in the eighteenth century included Chardins, Watteaus, Bouchers or any French pictures other than Claudes or Poussins until, later, those of Greuze and Vigée le Brun enjoyed a vogue. There is, however, a most important exception in Dr. Mead, one of the most distinguished physicians in the Europe of the 1740's. Very wealthy and hospitable, he spent a large part of his income in buying pictures and bronzes, with a taste sufficiently catholic to include Holbein and Rubens, Rembrandt and Franz Hals, Claude and Canaletto, Vandyck, Allan Ramsay and La Tour; and, when Watteau, in London and already consumptive, became his patient, Dr. Mead was perhaps the only man to recognise his greatness and became thereby a patron as well as a collector; apart from his support of Watteau, he was a patron in that he opened his collection to students while other collections remained closed to all but those who could afford the fantastically exorbitant fees (they were more than tips) to the servants and caretakers who herded the sightseer round the houses of the Great. Sir Andrew Fountaine, a friend of Swift, might, from his opportunities, have become a patron, since he knew nearly all the important artists of the time and was in a position to further their interests; but he preferred to be a virtuoso and, as Jonathan Richardson said,[1] he "out-Italianised the Italians themselves". Sir Andrew is one of the great collectors, in the same class as the Dukes of Portland and Bedford,

---

[1] Quoted by Whitley, *Artists and their Friends in England.*

Lord Bute,[1] Lord Lansdowne, Lord Radnor, Coke of Holkham and, later, Lord Stafford and Lord Grosvenor, Sir John Leicester, Sir George Beaumont and John Julius Angerstein. Horace Walpole is usually regarded as the prince of collectors, but some among his contemporaries saw him as a patron too; Thomas Patch, in 1772, dedicates his Life of Fra Bartolommeo to Walpole as "an Intelligent Promoter of the Fine Arts".

It seems clear that during the reign of George II an interest in the Fine Arts was spreading among the wealthy and educated; not only was the mere acquisition of pictures and statuary becoming more valuable as a source of social prestige, but it was considered desirable to possess, if not expert knowledge of, at any rate an articulate enthusiasm for, the objects acquired; most persons of quality learnt at least the jargon assiduously, if not always very intelligently, and some, impelled by a curiosity originally no more than modish, discovered the new pleasures of sensibility; indeed, it was not long before the Fine Arts came to be regarded as the only intellectual activity for which enthusiasm was not only permissible but desirable. It is not intended to suggest that the whole of the governing class suddenly, under George II, became devoted to the Arts, but an important section of it (not only in London) did begin to realise their existence; evidence of this is seen in the foundation, about 1732 or 1733, of the Society of Dilettanti.

Most of the members of this famous Society were young men and all of them retained throughout their

---

[1] Lord Bute was an early enthusiast for the Dutch School, of which he had the best collection before George IV.

lives that very active enthusiasm which gave the Society so great an influence on the taste of so many successive generations; whether they became Archbishops, Prime Ministers or Hell-Fire high priests,[1] they did not cease to be Dilettanti.[2] For a hundred years every enterprise of artistic or antiquarian importance, at home, in Greece, in Italy or in the Near East, was either undertaken or supported by the Society, as a whole or acting through individual members; more particularly were its activities devoted to the study of classical antiquities, and it was the money of the Dilettanti that made possible the excavations and the surveys of Gavin Hamilton or Stuart and Revett. Their scholarship was not always, perhaps, on the same level as that of Winckelmann, and their enthusiasm occasionally brought them into conflict with a less broad-minded public, as when, for example, Payne Knight published the famous *Priapeia* in 1786, which is an account of and discourse on the worship of Priapus; phallic rites were so little approved of by public opinion that the outcry caused Payne Knight to call in as many copies as possible of the work; it subsequently, of course, became extremely valuable. The Society also, in the person of Payne Knight, discredited Lord Elgin's Parthenon marbles, probably, as Sir Lionel Cust and Sir Sidney Colvin suggest, for fear lest the reputations of the Graeco-Roman collections of himself, Townley and Lord Lansdowne might suffer by comparison. Nevertheless, in spite of what might be considered occasional errors, the Society, with its

[1] *E.g.* Sir Francis Dashwood of Medmenham Abbey and West Wycombe, afterwards Lord Le Despencer.

[2] A very full account is given in *The History of the Society of Dilettanti*, compiled by Lionel Cust and edited by Sidney Colvin; printed for the Society and published in a limited edition in 1898.

energy, its enthusiasm and its wealth, became and remained for generations the most important body of its kind in Europe.

While almost all the noble and the wealthy were vigorously, if not always with discrimination, showing their enthusiasm for the Arts, the Court itself was slow in following; but it is untrue to say, as is often said, that it did not follow at all; George I and George II, admittedly, were almost entirely devoid of interest or taste; but the latter's consort, Caroline of Brandenburg-Ansbach, the one really interesting female member of the House before Queen Victoria, had, it is evident from her rediscovery of the Holbein portrait-drawings now at Windsor, and her enthusiasm for them, a discriminating eye and a considerable knowledge of such objects; her enthusiasm, which was real, was confined, however, to the enjoyment of possession rather than to the encouragement of production. But her son Frederick, Prince of Wales, abused by most historians, was an important figure among the virtuosi, dilettanti and cognoscenti[1] of the 1750's. He gave much assistance to individual artists and, according to Vertue, possessed taste, knowledge and enthusiasm; Vertue's evidence is not, perhaps, wholly reliable, as he was one of the Prince's especial protégés and owed much to his support, and it is chiefly from Vertue that we derive our knowledge of this side of his character; still, the Prince did at any rate realise the importance of the Royal Collections at Windsor and Hampton Court and was anxious that these should be as well catalogued and

[1] All three words were in use, "cognoscenti" tending to die out when "connoisseurs" came in, rather later. "Virtuoso" had a slightly professional implication, suggesting either a dealer or a painter. "Dilettante" later gave way to "amateur" and became weakened thereby.

cared for as they would have been had Charles I been on the throne; Vertue felt, after a conversation with him at Leicester House, that the Prince was capable of making an almost complete catalogue from memory and, if his memory failed at any point, of hurrying down to Hampton at a moment's notice to refresh it; this, on more than one occasion, he actually did in company with Vertue.

Frederick's son, George III, was no critic and not unusually enthusiastic, except for music; but he had a great anxiety to be associated with major artists, feeling that this might add lustre to his position; for this reason he took a very close personal interest with Sir William Chambers in the foundation of the Royal Academy, and retained his interest in, and authority over,[1] that body until his reason left him. When his son became Prince Regent, and later George IV, the Court may be said to have actually directed and formed Taste for the first time since the reign of Charles I, and certainly the Court became fashionable for the first time since 1688; fashion had always flocked to the Court of the Heir-Apparent, to Leicester House or its equivalent, and had been of the opposition; this precedent was followed until 1810, but after that date the Prince of Wales became virtually King and Carlton House the Court. The Regent was not only a collector of very great distinction but a patron such as had never, perhaps, been seen on the throne before; pictures in Buckingham Palace and furniture at Windsor show the collector, while the Castle itself as it now stands, and the remarkably successful career of Sir Thomas Lawrence,

[1] Cf. the King's action in causing Lawrence to be elected as an extra Associate of the Royal Academy in 1791.

show the patron at his most lavish; both Jane Austen and Sir Walter Scott also had reason to be grateful to that highly cultivated, if unreliable, king. With the exception of the Prince Consort, and one or two of Queen Victoria's children, none of the other Sovereigns nor their Consorts, nor any other member of this immensely prolific house, showed the faintest interest in any of the Arts, until modern times, though Queen Charlotte, it is said, was a pupil of Gainsborough; George III, for that matter, was a pupil of Joseph Goupy and Sir William Chambers and probably did possess some practical knowledge of painting and architecture.

Taste, however, though to a large extent deprived of what was in other countries the customary royal lead, was able to flourish by the variety and multiplicity of its other fertilising agents. In addition to the ardent and wealthy collectors and the occasional patrons, such as Lord Burlington, there was an unbroken succession throughout the century of professional artists who, by their actual achievements, were able to set widely followed fashions; Kent is, of course, one of the most important of these, followed in the next two generations by Sir William Chambers with his *chinoiserie*, by Robert Adam and Angelica Kauffmann, by "Athenian" Stuart and by the Gothic Wyatt. There were also the dealers and agents,[1] most of whom bought in Italy for collectors at home, like Irwin and Noël Desenfans and Fagan, who was the English Consul-General in Sicily and a very successful importer of Old Masters, and, most celebrated and successful of them all, Smith, the Consul in Venice, who did a flourishing trade in Cana-

---

[1] An illuminant on this subject is the Catalogue of the Sale of the Lansdowne Marbles by Messrs Christie in March 1930.

lettos. Besides these there were towards the end of the century a few important amateurs, neither collectors nor artists, who, by means of the treatise, the "open letter" or the article in the Press were able to give their ideas sufficient publicity to ensure, for a time, a fashionable following; apart from the professional criticism of Dr. Johnson and Wharton, the influence of Mrs Montagu, and in fact of all the Bluestockings, caused several minor revolutions in appreciation. The major revolution in the difficult and generally neglected art of seeing that followed the writings and public arguments of Gilpin, Mason, Payne Knight and Uvedale Price, had a longer life than most such revolutions in taste.[1]

[1] As late as the 1870's, it was possible to publish a guide-book with such a title as *Black's Picturesque Tourist in England.*

CHAPTER VII

THE AGE OF ADAM

THE indefinable yet rigid Rules of Taste laid down by
the Augustans under Queen Anne and George I maintained their supremacy for two-thirds of the eighteenth
century, not entirely unchallenged but strong enough,
with the support of Pope and Shenstone, Burlington,
Kent and Chambers, to resist the attacks of newer
schools and untraditional minds; strong enough, indeed,
to make successful revolution very difficult, for until
after the middle of the century the fashions that were
set by Authority were followed by almost everybody
and the mildest attempts at a revolution in architectural
taste, such as that of Batty Langley for the Gothic, were
accepted by so few that they were without any immediately perceptible effect on fashion; even Sir
William Chambers's attempt in the 1750's to effect a
revolution in favour of the Chinese was, as we have
seen, unsuccessful in face of the Palladian formality
of the school of Wren and the grandeur of Lenôtre,
for although Bridgeman and Kent introduced a flavour
of the romantic-picturesque into their gardens and parks
while George II was still on the throne they only did so
to accentuate by contrast the orthodoxy of the general
lay-out, and the revolution that actually established the
picturesque as the prevailing mode, with Mason and
Uvedale Price as its leaders, was really a part of the
romantic movement in the last decade of the century.

The Age of Adam

Yet even classic, Augustan taste suffered, in the 1770's and 1780's, if not a revolution at any rate a change, a dilution, through the influence of a newer school and of minds considered by the Burlingtonians unorthodox; the symptoms of the change were a tendency to design in two dimensions rather than three, or in line rather than in mass, to a lightened elegance, to what was pretty rather than imposing, to the feminine rather than to that masculine on which Inigo Jones had so strongly insisted. The leaders of this new school were the brothers Adam, but while consciously innovators they yet claimed to be the heirs of tradition, holding that the older school of Burlington and Chambers was not truly Classic but bastard Renaissance; what they claimed to do, and believed they had succeeded in doing, is stated by Robert Adam himself: "Architecture has already become elegant and more interesting. The parade, the convenience and social pleasures of life being better understood, are more strictly attended to in the arrangement and disposition of apartments. Greater variety of form, greater beauty in design, greater gaiety and elegance of ornament, are introduced into interior decoration: while the outside composition is more simple, more grand, more varied in its contour and imposes on the mind from the superior magnitude and movement of its parts."[1]

So Robert Adam compared his age with the age of Vanbrugh; and in this comparison may be seen all the new fashionable taste in decoration that we still associate with his name, a change that has outlasted many later and more violent changes and to which countless mass-produced chimney-pieces still bear witness; like

[1] *The Works of Robert and James Adam*, Part V, 1778.

115

all successful innovators, Adam has suffered from those who imitate him, but he changed the interiors of our houses as no one man has ever changed them since. We speak loosely of the "eighteenth century", assigning to it certain qualities, such as elegance, grace, a carefully controlled rococo gaiety, yet these qualities belong, not to the century, but to part of the reign of George III, and the century was more than half completed before he came to the throne. Our view of the century is thrown out of perspective by the intrusion into the picture of these brothers, whose work does indeed "impose on the mind", if not from its superior magnitude and movement, at least from its ubiquity and persistence.

Fully conscious of their superiority to their predecessors, the Adams had to defend themselves against much hostile criticism, especially from Sir William Chambers, who, citing his own Melbourne House, in Piccadilly,[1] maintained that he himself worked more in accordance with the style of the Ancients than did they, and even from the by no means undiscerning George III, who maintained that they had introduced too much of sweetness into their work, and likened it to confectionery.[2] Several years later the same criticism was made by the Rev. James Dallaway, in his day an authoritative critic, who observes "the Adelphi in the Strand may be classed with our publick works . . . considered as street-architecture, the whole wants solidity and the application of the plaster to imitate stone-work has certainly failed. The entrance into the Duke of North-

---

[1] Now Albany.

[2] An important clue to the nature of much eighteenth-century criticism is that no style was either attacked or defended on the grounds of its own merits, faults or individuality, but only in relation to Antiquity.

umberland's park at Sion is truly confectionery."[1]
Adam's answer to Chambers was to point out that most
"classical" work by architects since Inigo Jones, or
indeed since Palladio, was based on temples or the
ruins of temples, whereas his was based on a study of
the domestic architecture of Antiquity and, moreover,
that he and his brothers were the first to insist on the
distinction. His opinion of most modern architects was
low, as his travel diary shows; for in addition to dis-
liking almost anything in the French or Dutch tastes,
he says, "I am no admirer of the style of Palladio",[2] and
as a rule when that architect's work is referred to,
it is accompanied by such adjectives as "ill-adjusted",
"meagre", or "childish". Twenty years later, of course,
the uncritical dislikes of an enthusiast had become something more patient and tolerant, but the underlying
beliefs remained the same. In his *Works* he says of Vanbrugh that he "understood better than either (Inigo
Jones or Wren) the art of living among the Great. A
commodious arrangement of apartments was therefore
his peculiar merit. But his lively imagination scorned
the restraint of any rule in composition; and his passion
for what was fancifully magnificent prevented him from
discovering what was truly simple, elegant and sublime."[3]
Not, perhaps, a very good criticism of Vanbrugh, who
seldom achieved, or attempted to achieve, a commodious arrangement of apartments, but who did, at
Blenheim and Castle Howard, achieve the sublime; if,
that is to say, "sublime" is used with its particular implications, which, since Adam uses it in conjunction

---

[1] *Observations on English Architecture,* 1806.
[2] Quoted by Swarbrick, *Robert Adam and his Brothers,* 1915.
[3] *Works,* Part V.

with both "simple" and "elegant", may be a false assumption; this conjunction is a little surprising in an age when these epithets were used in a sense so meticulous and precise, when "sublime" almost always implied immensity and grandeur, and "elegant" was closely akin to the beautiful.[1]

If, however, the achievement of the simple was outside the plans of Vanbrugh or Kent, it was avowedly, so far as exteriors were concerned, the aim of the Adams; a sophisticated simplicity, not plainness, nor unadorned rusticity, but an exercise in restraint; proportion, a sense of light and air, an exact taste in the repetition of ornament and a meticulous insistence on the correctness of every detail were the means by which the change was carried out. Great houses, earlier in the century, were built, so to speak, behind their façades and their merit was considered to lie chiefly in their effect on the beholder as he approached; but the houses of the Adams are built round their interiors, they do not have *façade* in the scenic sense, and the outside, seen from any point, is the complement of the inside. Exceptions of course there are, such as Syon House, where a rather flimsy piece of confectionery leads one from the main road to two little Gothic lodges, beyond which a castellated, semi-Gothic mansion contains an unsuspected interior in Adam's most characteristic "grand" manner; but Adam's Gothic experiments are not many, and he can safely be typified by the always-quoted stock classical pieces. His name, in fact, has almost become generic, like that of Chippendale, for he has been so successful that we confuse the individual artist with the school that grew up

[1] See *ante*, Chapter IV.

round him, and the master is merged in the style.

The Adams were strong enough to modify, for the first time since they were formulated, the rules of Taste; not only were the rules changing, but they were becoming less rigid than in the days of Kent and "Capability" Brown; in Paris and Vienna, while similar changes were visible, the boundaries between what was permissible and what was not were as sharply defined as when Maria-Theresia or Louis XV were young; and in France, at least, this rigidity was to continue underneath many more changes, through the reign of Louis XVI, through the Directory and the Consulate, and even through the Restoration, to vanish with the democracy of Louis-Philippe. But in England the rules formulated in the post-revolution years, and rigidly enforced through the classical age of Queen Anne and the first two Georges, were relaxed when Kent was replaced by Adam and Angelica Kauffmann, when Addison gave way to Goldsmith, when prospects and vistas became landscapes and views, and "Capability" Brown was supplanted by Humphrey Repton and Uvedale Price, and the austerity of Inigo Jones, the genial masculinity of Wren, the virile dignity of Chambers went out of favour when Taste demanded the feminine grace of Adam. While not, in the derogatory sense, effeminate, the arts of painting, decoration, architecture and, to a large extent, poetry were markedly feminised from about the accession of George III to the end of the century, after which the Regency succeeded in combining incongruously but successfully a rigid austerity of line with a hearty vulgarity of adornment. With this quality of femininity went, naturally and as a complement, that of Sentiment, a slight, pretty, undisturbing Sentiment, innocent and, for preference, a little pathetic.

One effect of the new Sentiment is to be found in the increased importance of the Rustic Scene, and not only in its increased importance but in its popularisation; perhaps Thomson with his cycle of the Seasons inaugurated the new taste for rusticity, perhaps it was the new sentimental drama or perhaps, like so many other things, it can be attributed to the influence of Rousseau, but, whatever the primary cause may have been, the growing romantic tendency in the last quarter of the century sent out of fashion the pastorals of Pope and Vergil, shepherds and shepherdesses were translated into cottage-dwelling rustics and olive-groves became farm-yards; but yet the influence of Arcadia did not wholly disappear, for it continued as an important purifying, or idealising, agent since, if the Rustic Scene were to be in good taste, its innocence and its happiness should be stressed at the expense of its coarseness and its hardships. While the too-unsparing Hogarth was dismissed as being "low",[1] the sweet domesticities of Wheatley and the deodorised pig-styes of Morland found their way into every English home (where, generally speaking, they are still to be seen),[2] and we see Milkmaids, Benevolent Cottagers, Courting Swains and disconsolate Mariners' Widows issuing in their thousands from the print-shops of the 1780's and 1790's. A comparison which fairly shows the changed spirit of the times can be made between Wheatley's ever-popular *Cries of London*, wherein fish-wives and flower-sellers move through the streets with

[1] *I.e.* not elevating morally, and not in accordance with the principles of High, or Grand, Art. Cf. Reynolds, Discourse III.

[2] In engravings. The popularity of Morland has recently been confirmed by the prices made at the Joel sale at Christie's, June 1935.

the "sweet grace" of Lady Hamilton in her Romney days, and the series of the same subject by Marcellus Laroon three generations earlier, which are strong, individual, characteristic and convincingly true, though far from sweet. There is plenty of evidence to show that street life in London under George III was not more conspicuous for its innocence than it had been under William III, but in Laroon's day, when an interest in the humbler activities of mankind was not very marked, idealisation of such activities was less important because it was less necessary to work up an emotional interest in the poor; but to the contemporaries of Wheatley and Goldsmith yokels and slum-dwellers had become more romantic, no longer barbarian or criminal but now honest and hard-working, living lives in which simple joys alternated with heart-rending misfortunes, such as being seduced by the young squire or carried off by the press-gang. A certain idealising, therefore, of their appearance and their manners and customs was advisable if the sentimental myth were to continue.

And as the fashion for sentiment not only continued but spread into almost every activity of the mind, it was inevitable that painting should be affected by it; the effect in this case was to emphasise the influence of the Feminine, not in the vaguely prettifying way that we have seen in the case of Adamesque architecture, but in the definite emergence of the Female both as artist and as subject-matter, so that feminine influence was greater than at any previous time in the history of art in this country. Angelica Kauffmann is the obvious type of the contemporary female artist in that her success was due to her exploitation of feminine qualities (which would have availed the seventeenth-century Mary Beale but little) and to her appreciation of the feminine element in the fashionable Adamesque decoration; when Angelica depicts a scene with gods and goddesses it is not, at first sight, always very easy to pick out the gods, since, avoiding the more virile and Herculean deities, she reduces the others to a common femininity and gives Apollo the contours of a nymph. Most other decorative painters, besides Angelica, treat the nude in this way, so that in a series of the Youth of Achilles from Lansdowne House,[1] Cipriani gives the Hero a figure that would certainly render any disguise among the maidens in Scyros quite superfluous, at any rate when seen from behind.

Side by side with Angelica Kauffmann, Mrs Sharples, Mary Moser, and quiet, industrious Mrs Mee, a troop of distinguished female amateurs was busy, including Mrs Damer with her sculpture which sent Horace Walpole into polite transports of admiration, and Lady Diana Beauclerk, who abetted by Bartolozzi produced numbers of charming, playful cupids, plump and infinitely captivating. Children, in fact, as subject-matter, were second only to their mothers in popularity, as they had never been before but have been almost ever since; even Reynolds, the most masculine painter of the age, achieved his greatest popularity with Robinetta and the Infant Samuel, with Mrs Pelham and the Duchess of Devonshire rather than with Keppel or Lord Bath; and so it is with all his contemporaries; the weak, unstable Romney, vitiated by Emma Hart, Gainsborough with his rustling, iridescent grace,

[1] Catalogue of Lansdowne House Sale, by Messrs Christie, March 1930.

Hoppner with his coral necklaces and rouged vulgarity, Zoffany with his meticulous detail and more-than-silky silks, Allan Ramsay with the high elegance that is almost French, the smooth Cotes and the soft, delicately brilliant Russell, they all move through a world predominantly feminine, sufficiently feminine to be a little shocked when the Reverend William Peters, R.A., exhibited his sly, lascivious glimpses of Lydia's bosom; that, it was felt, was a little too Latin for English gentlewomen, whose bosoms were for the sole purposes of harbouring tender sentiments and nourishing their husband's children, and were not intended to be openly used as excitants.

It was an early symptom of the Romantic Age, for the well-ordered day of the Augustans had left little room for the intrusion of the Feminine; beyond a few gifted individual females, such as Caroline of Brandenburg-Ansbach, or Lady Mary Wortley Montagu or Sarah, Duchess of Marlborough, the sex continued to occupy, in the world of intellect, the place allotted them by man and long acquiesced in by themselves. But with the relaxing of the Rules came the assertive, though talented, troops of females bearing their pencils, their pens, their lexicons, painting, writing, translating, talking, surrounding Dr. Johnson or Mrs Montagu or Samuel Richardson, and provided that she were reasonably articulate, and very persistent, a measure of fame was certain for any woman whose adulators stressed sufficiently her sex. Mrs Elizabeth Clarke, Miss Kauffmann, Miss Burney, Miss Seward, Mrs Damer, Lady Diana Beauclerk, all achieved fame among their contemporaries, not because they excelled in their particular accomplishments but because they were females; and the Romantic spring already to be felt in the air was especially suited to the Feminine until it gave way to the high Romantic summer of the Regency, when the Male again outstripped her, though even then Sir Thomas Lawrence continued to allure in his peculiarly feminine way.

It follows that the men and women who lived in such a world demanded surroundings whose first quality should be elegance; first the Adams appeared, and conquered all competitors, subjugating even the virile and dignified Chippendale, whose fantastic rococo gains thereby in wit almost as much as it loses in virtue; and presently rich, sombre mahogany was banished, the delicate, painted drawing-rooms were filled with satinwood, light, flimsy and *chic*, and Miss Kauffmann and the Graces came into their own. Elegance, beyond doubt, was the prime achievement of the new taste; nevertheless, taste still posessed the necessary virtue of being able to laugh at itself, for as late as 1790 there was still demand for a new edition of William Wright's *Grotesque Architecture, or Rural Amusements*, which contained more than a score of designs in the highest fantasy, for Primitive Huts, Chinese Grottoes, Triumphal Cascades, Romantic Arches (with or without Cascades), Moresque Pavilions, Turkish Mosques, and Hermitages oriental, rural, summer, winter, modern or antique; they are the link between Pope's Villa and the Brighton Pavilion, and are as important as they are amusing, for however self-consciously elegant or pedantically Grecian taste might become, so long as there remained a desire to be diverted or a demand for the witty and amusing, so long would there continue to be style; slight and impermanent foundations these are, truly; in fact, they are not foundations at all so much as guiding factors, important because ridicule is so potent an agent of criticism. The *Chinoiseries* and the *Rural Amusements* are the witty comments on the follies of the humourless, and but for them, taste might very easily have become stationary and remained lifeless and sterile.

There were, after all, many dangers to be guarded against; the age was becoming so refined and delicate, so elegant and so genteel, that sentiment and fancy became the sovereign qualities, the fanciful particularly being in demand; to this, the revolution in industrial methods directly contributed, by causing machines to be invented which enabled the craftsman to produce marvels of pretty dexterity with comparative ease, and by the production of substitute materials, of which stucco and cast-iron, though the most extensively used, were far from being the only ones; there was, for example, Coade's Artificial Stone, the manufactory for which was founded in 1769.[1] The advantage of this burnt artificial stone over the natural was its alleged property of resistance to frost and thence its peculiar suitability for garden ornaments and for tombs and monuments in churchyards.[2] The firm's catalogue for 1784 gives a good idea of its activities, for it includes a River God 9 feet high, with an Urn through which a stream of water may be carried, for one hundred guineas; an Elegant Tomb for a churchyard, for sixty

[1] In the Advertisement to their Catalogue for 1784 they mention "the period of 15 years since this . . . manufactory has been erected".

[2] The cheapness and economy of this historically important manufacture are remarked on approvingly by Farington, *Diary*, vii. 277. A full account is given in *The Connoisseur*, lxxxii. 81. Cf. also Bibliographical Society's *Transactions*, no. xv (1920).

guineas; a Sarcophagus with figures, for thirty guineas; Psyche, "fitted up with spring-tubes for lights", for five guineas; and a series of busts including Homer, Marcus Aurelius, Cicero, Vandyck, Edward VI, Queen Elizabeth, Lord Chatham and the Madonna, ranging from three guineas for Queen Elizabeth to fifteen shillings for the Madonna. The firm was also able to supply inexpensive vases, pedestals, coats of arms, frizes (*sic*), pinnacles, chimney-pieces, balusters and "rustic" stones for archways.

These catalogues of Coade Statuary and of Rural Amusements to be ordered direct from the manufacturer are significant of new standards in criticism, marking an early appearance of the cheap, mass-produced "work of art"; the difference between this and the Augustan and Burlingtonian standards is not a change of kind, for the decorators and gardeners of 1790 were quite as consciously, though very differently, mannered as their predecessors of 1740, but a decline in thoroughness or, which may be regarded as the same thing, a freedom from pedantic adherence to rule, for while formerly ruins, grottoes, temples or ornaments were designed in relation to the surrounding scenery or in illustration of a literary Idea, they were now selected from a book of patterns, and appraised on their own particular merits, as seen through the spectacles of fashion, rather than on their suitability for a given function in a given setting. It may well be objected that a Roman ruin in a Georgian garden is in any case unsuitable, and so it is if a garden be regarded simply as a selected and tidied piece of natural scenery; but if a garden be regarded as a work of art made by man for the enjoyment and edification of man, then such objects are seen as apt allusions to man's intellectual, spiritual or emotional experiences, to be paralleled with classical quotations or couplets from Pope. The wise Augustan rule that man's reason be regarded as superior to Nature's savagery made it essential that the hand of the architect and the sculptor should be everywhere visible, but in a later and more romantic generation the depths of reason shallowed to a mere fashionable pursuit and in due course were forgotten in a new, Wordsworthian philosophy.

But before that philosophy had completed its victory, or even entered the battle, there is visible a struggle during the last quarter of the century between gardeners with their sophisticated, picturesque naturalism and the decorators with their continued insistence on reference to the achievements of man, particularly in either the Classical or the Gothic past; the decorators were ultimately defeated by the gardeners, but nevertheless they succeeded in inventing a formula that has outlasted the memory of their opponents; inheritors of a tradition with which they could not sympathise, they were yet fully conscious of the new spirit of light and sensuous elegance, an elegance spidery in its delicate fineness, and refined till all plastic feeling had gone; there could indeed be no great plastic feeling in an age which began with Adam and ended with Flaxman, nor could the sense of architecture find a place in its scheme of decoration (it did not always find a very clearly defined place in its architecture either, for that matter). Ingenuity in arabesque, inventiveness in detail, a delicate taste in ornament are dangerous qualities and such as are apt to run wild when control is slackened; with the astonishing perfection of the Adam school in decorating flat surfaces and in devising elegant objects to hang from or stand against such flat surfaces, the architect declined inevitably into the decorator. Not, perhaps, a "decline" so long as the Adams themselves were in authority, but rather a development in a new direction; there could hardly be decline when such felicity of invention was supported by a perfection of craftsmanship such as they were able to command; the craftsmanship in fact continued unimpaired for more than half the next century, but inventiveness, by slowly gaining the victory over sense, ceased to be the servant of the housebuilder and became his master.

Painting also, like the other arts, contributed to the new elegance; and, if the function of the picture-maker be to produce articles of furniture, the contribution was entirely successful. English pictures are generally more easily appreciated if they be presented as objects in an inhabited room rather than as exhibits in a gallery, and if seen among the surroundings for which they were painted, gentlemen's pictures in a gentleman's house, as much part of the fittings of that house as the chairs and tables and plate, to be regarded primarily as embellishment and not as material for the critic to dissect. While the famous "good manners" of English painting under Reynolds and Richard Wilson were well supported by Adam, even though he and his followers did interpret the code a trifle freely,[1] the succeeding painters, in spite of Sir Joshua, anticipated the vulgarity and cheapness that the builders were still able to avoid, for Romney, Hoppner, Beechey and Lawrence are not quite worthy of Henry Holland, Nash

[1] Cf. the manners of Bath, which are perfect, with the Adelphi, which is a little self-conscious and genteel.

or Soane. There were still a few original painters, like Opie, Fuseli or Blake, but the majority, ardent in their admiration of the Classical at the expense of the Renaissance, succeeded in focussing their attention on only one aspect of their model and, reacting from the scientific temper of the Renaissance, saw in the Classical the triumph of simplicity, or, in other words, they saw it in two dimensions instead of in three; this limited vision, combined with a lack of distinguished leadership, is responsible for the poor quality of English painting at the close of the century. Raeburn alone, apart from the three just mentioned, despite his commonplace mind and photographic eye, resisted the prevailing fashion and is still able to attract us occasionally by a display of what most of his contemporaries lacked —style; this prevailing fashion, as followed by Hoppner and his contemporaries, may be described as a combination of the general effect of Reynolds with an extreme simplification of form, a foretaste of the Neo-Classic already established across the Channel as a result of the Revolution, and its relation to its pretended source could be seen if a bas-relief by Flaxman were fixed to a column of the Parthenon.

The words of Robert Adam, quoted early in this chapter, were in fact applicable, not only to architecture, but to all the arts, for all of them had become certainly more "elegant", if not more interesting; but whether the suggested decline in architecture and decoration, leaving painting aside, is seen as due to the Adams themselves or to their followers, it is fairly evident that one cause of it may be found in the examples the brothers set; two, especially, were dangerous. In their street-planning they pointed clearly to the time when the builder should take the place of the architect; and by their introduction of such substitute materials as cast iron and Liardet's stucco they made it easy for an indifferent building to renew a false and misleading charm with a fresh coat of paint. Their more conservative predecessors, like Kent or Isaac Ware, had used bricks and stone with a strong sense of the special qualities of their medium, a sense which had been developed by the inheritance of a native tradition strong enough to anglicise, and sufficiently elastic to modernise, all the successive introductions from other climates and past centuries; moreover, before the Industrial Revolution, both the materials for their use and the patrons for whom they worked exacted a standard of solid strength which a later and less conservative age thought a trifle uncouth. This revulsion from the so-called uncouth affected literature with the weak beginnings of romanticism, painting with an irrelevant and literary sentiment, architecture with a desire to be decorative before anything else, and manners with a passion for sensibility.

In the Abbey Church of Dorchester, in Oxfordshire, is a memorial to a young lady, a Mrs Sarah Fletcher, who, her nerves being too delicately spun, died a Martyr to Excessive Sensibility, on the 7th June 1799, at the age of 28. No doubt quantities of other young wives who had brutal husbands died of Excessive Sensibility, just as their sisters who had no husbands at all died of Declines. The gentle smile of Jane Austen helped to discourage that fashion, but it took the French Revolution and the Napoleonic Wars to kill Gentility in architecture; the Regency checked for a time the decline, but the Industrial Revolution left results more permanent than anything inspired by George IV. Horace Walpole, who laughed at most things, laughed at this extreme attention paid to fashion in a "projected History of Good Breeding, in ten volumes",[1] which, of course, proceeded no further than the Advertisement, in which he proposes to treat of Good Breeding in general, of Ceremonies, of Visits, of Bows and Curtesies, of Duels and whether it be more honourable to be beat by one that is no Gentleman than to fight him, of the folly of being well-bred to persons in want or affliction, of the Duty of dancing and giving Balls; of whether Compliments are Lies, and whether Bishops should talk bawdy at christenings; of how impertinent a Peeress may be, and at what age a handsome woman should begin to grow Civil; of the institution of Duchesses and the incorporation of School-mistresses; of snuff-boxes, illegitimate Princes, Marriages, Maidenheads and Widows. As the punctilio of Walpole's youth had gradually lost its meaning by exaggeration, so the earlier good manners of the Arts suffered in the same way, and in the same way were lost to sight beneath the growing affectations. But while fashion was losing its power to guide steadily in a given direction, it yet retained its old prestige; the heading of Chapter VIII in the "History of Good Breeding" was to be "Nothing so ill-bred as to persist in anything that is out of fashion. Taste and Fashion synonymous Terms."

[1] *Collected Works*, vol. i.

CHAPTER VIII

THE GREEKS AND THE ROMANS

TASTE and fashion are certainly to a very large extent synonymous terms, for when it becomes fashionable to profess a taste for the arts fashion is able to dictate to her followers what line their taste should take; while Taste was forming, early in the century, there was but little room for tastes and indeed the prevailing orderliness of mind, the dislike of enthusiasm, made the excentric seem almost repugnant, for when each manifestation of the human mind and talents had its prescribed form, and when those prescribed forms had been proved satisfactory by the practice of authoritative masters, it seemed idle to search for other forms and impertinent to question orthodox practice; no fashion has at any time been universally followed, and the orthodox has always had its opposition, but until the day of the Adams any departure from the Rules was confined to individuals and condemned to relative sterility; thus while Batty Langley had his Gothic followers he set no widespread Gothic fashion, and, while Chambers's Chinese amused a few, pagodas were generally frowned on as being fanciful; only Authority itself could sanction the fanciful, and it is probable that if Pope had not built a grotto there would have been no grottoes before the end of the century; similarly, Lord Burlington condemned the Gothic and that style had to wait a generation until Authority in the person of

Horace Walpole sanctioned its use.

Once, however, the Rule of Taste had become a tradition it began to mitigate its severity and allowed a variety of tastes to become fashionable. It was felt that England had demonstrated her ability to use the classical idiom and had established her ambitious claim to be as civilised as France, and as the victories of Marlborough had aroused that ambition, now the victories of Chatham and the triumphs of the Seven Years' War filled her with a belief in her own real greatness that not even the American rebellion could shake; she took her place proudly as the first among European nations in war and statecraft, and was able to accept, as a matter of course and as rightly due to her, the tribute of anglomania paid so enthusiastically by Paris and by those parts of Europe that regarded Paris as their intellectual capital. This self-confidence, this realisation of an ambition achieved, bred not surprisingly a resentment against the continued control of Authority over self-expression or, to put it less strongly, awakened the actual or potential patron to the realisation that an English painter, poet or architect could express himself worthily without reference to France or Italy and even, upon occasion, without reference to Antiquity. The intensely personal and English idiom of Gainsborough would have been thought vulgar forty years earlier, because he could have been related to no rule that had ever been laid down and his ex-centricity would have been an insurmountable obstacle; but he had the good fortune to reach maturity at a time when rules were losing their tradition of infallibility and were no longer the sole guardians of national dignity against the attacks of enthusiasm.

The Rule of Taste

This change was part of no violent revolution, but was a symptom of that tendency, so revolutionary in its effects, which the text-books call the Romantic movement and which we may describe as the gradual ascendancy of liberalism over dictatorship or, at any rate, over oligarchy. The two forces waged a long war, in England as in the rest of the civilised world; the American rebels, John Wilkes, "Junius" and Tom Paine gave voice and action to the growing feeling in favour of individualism, while George III, Burke and the well-managed machinery of the Constitution represented the forces of order and control; the conflict had its political, intellectual and emotional aspects and in its early stages the partisans were clearly divided into those who thought they loved Liberty and those who knew they dreaded it. But the French Revolution plunged the minds of all men into a confusion, either of fear or of enthusiasm, which rendered clarity of thought impossible and which we can now see as one of the prevailing characteristics of the "Romantic" age, the age in which enthusiasms began to take the place of standards.

It is characteristic of English conservatism that the political and social standards should have changed but slowly, while the arts, because they had a much shorter tradition behind them, were more deeply affected and were thrown into a confusion from which they have not yet wholly emerged, and which may be illustrated by a paradox drawn from France. It should be borne in mind that the word Democratic, though not new,[1] was hardly used except as an expression of loathing or fear and that the word Romantic, used at least since

[1] Dr. Johnson quotes in the *Dictionary* examples of its use by Locke and Sir William Temple.

the time of Addison to suggest the absurd, improbable, chimerical, wild or false, was in the last years of the eighteenth century widely applied to the great destructive forces of the time and "romanticks" were very generally identified with revolutionaries; yet, and here is the paradox, the art most closely associated with the revolution in France is the art of Jacques-Louis David; the expression of the dynamic enthusiasm of the Jacobins is entrusted to the clear-headed intellectual who saw painting in the static terms of sculpture; but in the Europe of the 1790's it is possible to explain even the most improbable associations, and it may be presumed that the youthful David, while Louis XV was still reigning, derived his first incitement to the Classic from the published results of the German Winckelmann's industrious excavations, for, sick of the languid and exhausted tradition of Pater, Lancret and Boucher, with their endless fêtes and gallantries, and sick too of the social system which they typified, he felt the art of republican Rome to be the most fitting expression of the republican France that he hoped one day to see; others who felt as he did and actually accomplished the Revolution were less clear-headed and, confusing republican with imperial Rome, found themselves committed to an imperial France. But before that unlooked-for development took place, it is possible to hear, through all the noise and tumult of 1789, the pickaxe of Winckelmann helping to demolish the Bastille.

This seeming paradox, this confused association of the classical with the revolutionary or, to use a milder word, with the romantic, is very marked in England for at least two decades before the French Revolution, and the authority of the Renaissance, as personified in Sir

William Chambers and Sir Joshua Reynolds, the Rules, as incorporated in the Royal Academy, were losing a little of their power before the growing influence of Greece; though it would perhaps be truer to call it the Grecian rather than Greece, for the distinction between Greek, Roman and Graeco-Roman was not at that time very clearly established. In fact, for the majority of collectors in the eighteenth century the distinction hardly existed at all, and when in the early years of the nineteenth century certain critics endeavoured to point out the differences they were opposed with considerable hostility on the part of Authority; the argument and dissension produced by the Elgin Marbles is a case in point. Were these, which the nation was being urged to acquire, genuine Greek sculpture or were they to be pronounced spurious? While the artists in general, and Benjamin Robert Haydon in particular, insisted that they were genuine, it was natural that the weightiest authoritative opinion should pronounce them to be, at the best, but Roman; for Authority in such a matter meant the great collectors. Long before the purchase from Lord Elgin of these Parthenon marbles[1] certain enthusiastic antiquarians like Lord Shelburne, Charles Townley or Thomas Hope were beginning to entertain secret doubts as to whether everything they had bought as "Greek" from the dealers in Rome or through Gavin Hamilton[2] was in fact Greek, and should Lord Elgin appear to be justified in all he claimed for his collection their own purchases might begin to look like expensive mistakes; as it happened,

[1] The marbles were bought from Lord Elgin for the British Museum in 1816.

[2] Cf. Messrs Christie's Catalogue of Sale of Lansdowne Marbles, March 1930.

although they had the very substantial support of
Payne Knight,[1] who wielded in his day an authority
equal to that of Ruskin later, their opposition was in
vain.

This vicarious victory of Lord Elgin is the first really
damaging blow at the Dictators' continued authority,
but the ground had already been partly prepared by
some of the more clear-sighted of the Dilettanti, who
were inclined to differ from the orthodox view which
held that the art of Antiquity, like that of the Renaissance, derived primarily from Rome and which regarded Rome as the mother of all civilisation with a
vague, dim background called sometimes Latium and
sometimes Etruria. As far back as 1762 James "Athenian"
Stuart and Nicholas Revett had published their great
Antiquities of Athens, the success of which was largely
responsible for the "Grecian Gusto" that, before the
end of the century, had taken the place of the Renaissance as the most desirable form for domestic architecture to take; and one of the most enthusiastic
supporters of this Athenian undertaking was Sir William
Hamilton, one of the relatively small number of collectors able to add to enthusiasm a scholarly discrimination. As Plenipotentiary at Naples for thirty-six years[2]
he had ample opportunity for indulging his archaeological inclinations, which were strong, and for apply-
ing to the results his critical powers, which were badly
needed. Excavating was a popular diversion of the
time, following the fashion set by Winckelmann, and
since many of the excavators possessed little equipment

[1] See his evidence before the Select Committee of the House of
Commons on the Elgin Marbles.

[2] From 1764 to 1800; though he left Naples for Palermo with the
Court in 1798.

beyond optimism and credulity, it was desirable that somebody should claim authority to distinguish between the real and the imitation and, having rejected the many very skilful forgeries, should attempt a classification of the remainder. While Gavin Hamilton in Rome was excavating and exporting marbles and bronzes, Sir William Hamilton devoted himself to the study of the vases that were being removed in great quantities from tombs all over the Neapolitan territories. It had long been the custom to label all such vases "Etruscan", especially among the students before Winckelmann, possibly because, as Sir William rather spitefully suggests, "Buonaroti and Gori, being themselves Tuscans, meant to do honour to their native country by attributing such Elegant Works of Art to the Etruscans; and subsequent Authors adopted that opinion".[1] He himself, as he admits, when he first began to collect, adopted that opinion; but his considerable knowledge of Greek philology and mythology gave him the idea that these vases might have a Grecian rather than an Etruscan origin. Such a view at that time was opposed to most European opinion, and particularly to the opinion of those responsible for the Grand Ducal collections at Florence, but Sir William's experience, enthusiasm and knowledge enabled him to prove his case and to cause his view to be accepted. He speaks with authority, not only as a "passionate lover of the Arts", but as one who has for very many years "particularly attended to this sort of Antiquity", and who has a rare regard for the ascertainable truth; "were I", he says, "to report all I have

[1] Introduction to Sir William Hamilton's *Collection of Engravings from Ancient Vases*, published by Tischbein in Naples, 1791, and dedicated to the Earl of Leicester (2nd Marquess Townshend), President of the Society of Antiquaries.

heard relative to these sepulchres it would make a volume, but as I have by long experience found how very difficult it is to get at truth I am resolved to relate only what I have seen myself and say nothing rather than hazard an untruth".

As the years passed, and his collections expanded, Sir William Hamilton found it necessary to weed out; shiploads of vases were sent to England; some were sold, with great benefit to the excavator, some were presented to institutions; many were acquired by the British Museum, others, which he himself had bought, such as the "Warwick" and "Portland" vases, were sold to private collectors. But although the labours of Winckelmann and Hamilton, of Stuart and Revett, prepared the ground, and despite the implications of "Grecian Gusto", it was not before the early 1790's that Italy began to give place to Greece in the estimation of the orthodox man of taste. An example of such is Josiah Wedgwood, who, whatever his later influence, was certainly not at the beginning of his career a precisian for the Greek; when he rebuilt his house and founded his new works in 1770 he called it Etruria.

Etruria Hall, when Wedgwood had altered it and made it habitable, was an imposing and stately mansion, in which "capacity existed everywhere for the decorative effects of stained-glass and terra-cotta bas-reliefs"; [1] the situation was somewhat bleak and exposed, but Nature, however forbidding, was but a poor match for "Capability" Brown and his followers; as a contributor to the *Gentleman's Magazine* in 1794 says of Etruria, "the hills and valleys are here beautifully formed, but owe much to the improvement of Art", which doubt-

[1] Eliza Meteyard, *Life of Josiah Wedgwood*, 1866.

less they did, for twenty-five years earlier Wedgwood's landscape gardener had "gathered the moorland springs into a lake, breaking the levels here and there with knolls, and planting generously"; [1] and the planting went on for many years. The clay in which this little Eden grew was turned, in the factory down by the canal beyond the house, into those lovely shapes which captivated alike the Irish nobility, to whom they were introduced by Lord Bessborough, and the Quakers, who followed the example of the wealthy and important Mr Barclay in buying quantities of the simple, delicate cream-ware for their dining-tables, as well as everyone between those two extremes, and which was exported almost all over the world.

In time Wedgwood too came to regard Greece as a worthier source of inspiration than Etruria, for like others he was beginning to find that while Etruria really meant very little, Greece meant already a great deal. Probably the chief cause of this conversion is his lasting friendship with "Athenian" Stuart, who frequently lent him objects from his own collection to be interpreted or translated into the new ware. Wedgwood seldom set himself to reproduce antique vases exactly, but rather to adapt them, though certain very important individual vases he did copy, as for example the Barberini (or Portland), which was brought to England by Sir William Hamilton towards the end of 1784 and bought almost immediately, though in the greatest secrecy, by the Duchess Dowager of Portland. Wedgwood at once began his long attempt to reproduce it, but not till the autumn of 1789 was the perfect copy accomplished. As his business prospered an increas-

---

[1] Eliza Meteyard, *Life of Josiah Wedgwood*, 1866.

ingly large sum was spent every year in books for the use of his modellers; by pressing into his services the finest books issued in Rome or Venice, in Paris or Amsterdam, by using the genius for design of Flaxman or Adam, and by calling up all antiquity, Wedgwood was able to influence and dominate an age. His responsibility for the neo-Grecian in the arts other than architecture is as great in England as is that of J. L. David and the French Revolution in the rest of Europe.

The important point, however, is that this neo-Classic art is not antagonistic to, but complementary to, the Romantic and that taste for ten years before 1800 and twenty years after became increasingly a fusion of the two. Blake had his visions as romantic as those of Turner and painted them in forms as classical as those of Flaxman; Wyatt built first in the classic manner and ended with Fonthill and Ashridge; Nash built Regent Street and the Regent's Park Terraces and followed them up with the Pavilion at Brighton. The Grecian of Flaxman and Sir John Soane was balanced by the Gothic of Pugin and Sir Jeffrey Wyatville, and the medievalism of Carter and Horace Walpole by the archaeology of Sir William Hamilton; and Lady Hamilton's Grecian eurhythmics were imitated by romantic ladies wearing Marie-Stuart ruffs and sleeves. Henry Holland's Carlton House was quite as expressive of the age as Nash's Pavilion, or Beckford's Fonthill as Thomas Hope's Deepdene. This fusion of tastes or fashions is well exemplified by a prayer-book in the British Museum bound by Edwards of Halifax for Queen Charlotte; its cover is decorated with Etruscan ornaments, surrounded by a Greek key-pattern border and, in a lunette, a Gothic ruin adds its romantic flavour.

The Rule of Taste

While we to-day can look back on the 1790's and early 1800's as a time of the well-ordered fusion of several different methods of expression, we see that fusion as confusion if we look a little further back and contrast it with the order that prevailed before, when there was only one fashion to be *generally* followed at any one moment and when revolts against that fashion were confined to enthusiasts or to what would now be called "modernists"; the rules of Correct Taste had guarded successfully for nearly a century against what was Incorrect, and the Renaissance-Palladian idiom had become during that period traditional and formed the canon of orthodoxy; during that same period a certain form of government and a certain organisation of society had also become traditional, in the form of an oligarchic aristocracy. While the aristocratic social régime was left unattacked for many years to come, the political régime was constantly attacked and would have been overthrown (probably by Pitt himself) had not a European war diverted men's attention and made national defence more urgent than political argument. Nevertheless, the system was becoming increasingly discredited, as we can see from the extremely important effect on public opinion wrought by John Wilkes and by the Letters of "Junius".[1] With the growing feeling for a more popular, a more liberal, form of government the alarmingly romantic idea of Democracy became increasingly attractive but it had the curious, though not wholly unexpected, effect of turning the minds of many theorists in the direction of Athens and the Greek city-states. Simultaneously the Arts also underwent a revulsion of

[1] Tom Paine is of far less importance, by reason of the violence of his opinions, which aroused the instinctive English antipathy to force.

feeling against the existing order, for the Palladian-Renaissance tradition had come to be wholly identified with the anti-popular political system which it so exactly expressed; but the demand for a more liberal aesthetic theory meant little more than a desire for anything rather than the existing rules, and while many worked for a more complete revival of the Antique and an association of the Arts with politics, as was being attempted in France, almost as many others wished to go no further back than a pre-Renaissance existence, and found their mind's satisfaction in medievalism. But while in France, so soon as the first tumult of the Revolution was over, art and politics combined in a new and imperial dictatorship, establishing the absolute authority of "the Greeks and the Romans",[1] in England there was no dictator, and schools and academies no longer troubled themselves about a policy; the Horace Walpole-medievalists urged in one direction, the Flaxman-classicalists in another and the "naturalists" in a third. There was room for Fuseli as well as for Flaxman, for Lawrence as well as for Chantrey; the town flocked to hear Mrs Siddons declaim Shakespeare as if he were Sophocles, and idolised her for her statuesque dignity as it did Macready for his romantic fire; yet it was not only her power of incarnating the Muse of Tragedy that gave Sarah Siddons her fame, for all, from Hazlitt downwards, were overwhelmed by her mastery of every emotional effect from pathos to horror. English neo-classicism never wholly freed itself from the emotions, but romanticism was a long time in throwing off the last trace of classic authority.

What, for example, could be more romantic than

[1] See Clive Bell, *Landmarks in Nineteenth-Century Painting*, 1927.

The Rule of Taste

Erasmus Darwin's presentation of botanic science?[1] Or more Augustan than his Pope-like metre? True, the manner of Pope was already rather *démodé*, but the mixture of natural philosophy with botany lessons called for something a little more conventional, more academic, than the modern manner could supply. The philosophy of the *Botanic Garden* was Darwin's own, the botany was taken from Linnaeus; the sentiments were sometimes his, and sometimes those of the perhaps justly annoyed Miss Anna Seward, who held that insufficient acknowledgment had been made to her inspiration of his Muse. Even their close association with the neighbouring Wedgwoods could not cause that Derby and Lichfield coterie to be taken with the seriousness that Miss Seward and Dr. Johnson would have liked; "one of those harmonious virgins", Horace Walpole calls her, and she has never been released from the burden of that double reproach, though her harmonies are not wholly negligible and her continued virginity was due to no squeamish reluctance on her part, as Dr. Darwin knew. "All tinkling and tinsel," Miss Mitford says, "a sort of Dr. Darwin in petticoats." Yet Darwin, by the force of his originality and his deep love of plants and flowers and trees, can conjure into animation all the inanimate world and invest with humanity the humblest or the most minute of Nature's vegetable creation.

> So the lone Truffle, lodged beneath the earth,
> Shoots from paternal roots the tuberous birth.[2]

[1] *The Economy of Vegetation* was published in 1792, forming Part I of the *Botanic Garden*, and *The Loves of the Plants*, forming Part II, was published three years earlier; the third volume of his Poetical Works, *The Temple of Nature*, was published in 1803, the year after Darwin's death.

[2] *The Origin of Society*, canto ii.

144

He has a complete mastery of Augustan rhythm and epithet, as well as a sense of dignity that at once removes the truffle from its mere swine-rootled edibility on to the same plane as man himself. It is precisely this power of translating one order of Creation into terms of another, or of expressing all Creation in terms of Man, the only terms that we ourselves can understand, that impelled his grandson one step nearer the key to creation itself.

> The wakeful Anther in his silken bed
> O'er the pleased Stigma bows his waxen head,[1]

is as scientific as any Linnaean could wish, but it remained for Darwin to suggest that plants, like ourselves, take pleasure in the process of procreation; yet the amorous, romantic colouring is toned down by a reticence of epithet and a regularity of metre that indicate skill of a high order. Even when he surrenders to the convention of his day, by interpolating a loyal reference to the Throne, he can make his Sovereign as human as any plant, yet still invest him with dignity:

> So sits enthroned in vegetable pride
> Imperial Kew by Thames's glittering side.
>
> .   .   .   .
>
> Sometimes retiring from the public weal
> One tranquil hour the ROYAL PARTNERS steal;
> Through glades exotic pass with step sublime,
> Or mark the growths of Britain's happier clime.[2]

A scientist whose researches were of the greatest benefit to Wedgwood, an imaginative thinker whose mind anticipated the beliefs of Charles Darwin, a philosopher who observed all Nature, a poet who saw spiritual

---

[1] *Ibid.*   [2] *The Economy of Vegetation*, canto iv.

beauty in a truffle, an Augustan body encasing a romantic soul, Erasmus Darwin is typical of the closing years of his century. So, too, in his smaller range of activity, is Thomas Stothard; now Grecian, now Gothic; at one moment all for antiquity, at another wholly medieval; traditional in his unquestioning admiration of Greek sculpture, he yet considered that "several of the monumental effigies of Great Britain were examples of a pure and beautiful style of art",[1] though he adds that "the want of knowledge in perspective and chiaroscuro showed an uneducated state of the art".

The Greeks and the Romans exercised their authority even in England, but they were far from absolute, for Horace Walpole and Bishop Percy had rediscovered respectively the architecture and the ballads of the Middle Ages, and with each year everything romantic received a greater and more devoted attention; the sublime conceptions of John Martin on canvas, for example, were praised by people who twenty years earlier were admiring only the sculpturesque designs of Poussin or the well-ordered landscapes of Claude. Stothard himself praised the grandeur of "Belshazzar's Feast" and especially admired the supernatural light which Martin called out from the writing on the wall; but he quarrelled with the bad drawing of the figures, which did not accord with the canons of Classical art. With equal paradox, his romantic tendencies caused him to admire Mrs Fitzherbert, his classical to admire Mrs Siddons, "the two greatest beauties he had ever seen". Mrs Fitzherbert was "dazzling in her attractions", the latter was commanding, "with nothing that was common about her"; "no one", said Stothard, "could

[1] Anna Eliza Bray, *Life of Thomas Stothard, R.A.,* 1851.

146

have entertained a light thought in the presence of Mrs Siddons". So successfully did Mrs Siddons create the impression of being an incarnated Muse, that her Olympian dignity never, for one instant, left her; so that Stothard could actually describe her as being "entirely free from affectation . . . she was content to be natural".

Thus, while Stothard urged "a sedulous study of Antique sculpture to all young artists", he also impressed on them the usefulness of a study of Gothic antiquity, and set the example himself; his great picture of Chaucer's Canterbury Pilgrims was widely celebrated in his own day and for long after, and even to-day is very popular. Antiquity he reverenced, the Middle Ages he studied, his own contemporaries he could praise: as he did Turner in all his different phases, or Callcott, or Harlow who, "had he been spared, would have become one of the first portrait-painters that this country has ever produced"; this verdict may perhaps err on the side of generosity, as had there been no Lawrence there might have been no Harlow. But the Renaissance he mistrusted and misunderstood, despite his admiration for the colour of Rubens. As an example of his interest in the Middle Ages, he described as commendable the accuracy of medieval monumental effigies, in that one could "rely on the truth of their portraits", because they did not represent their kings in Roman armour with full-bottomed wigs; the student of iconography will realise how incautious a statement that is. Nevertheless, however uncritical may have been Stothard's classical tastes, or incomplete his medievalism, his desire to see the best in both worlds is wholly characteristic of his generation.

Most artists at this time could create with equal ease in either style, and all critics could praise equally the Grecian or the medieval, for either could be made to accord with modern tastes; few, however, were sufficiently open-minded to criticise the critics on whom most of their opinions were inevitably founded. Henry Fuseli, Swiss by birth and English by adoption, is perhaps the only Academic professor who is consistently caustic about the sources from which his professional learning is derived. He knew, for instance, that our knowledge of the sculpture of Antiquity was confused (more so in his day than in ours), and of the painting was almost nothing; for what little knowledge we had of the latter was based on Roman historians; and his opinion of those historians was poor, though his acquaintance with them was considerable; he knew his Quintilian and his Pliny, could quote much Cicero, a little of the elder and the younger Philostrates, Lucian and Pausanias the Cappadocian and could refer often enough to Aelian, to Pollux and to several others (of whom he said they may be consulted with advantage by the man of taste and neglected without much loss by the student). On these foundations Fuseli could build up, in his Academy lectures[1] on Ancient Art, elaborate criticisms of antique painting, yet say of Pliny that he "was rather desirous of knowing much than of knowing well",[2] that he is "credulous, irrelevant and ludicrous"; that his standard is either the grapes which imposed on the birds or the curtain which deceived Zeuxis; of Pausanias the Cappadocian that "he

[1] Fuseli was Professor of Painting at the Royal Academy 1799–1825. Keeper, 1804–25. Elected R.A., 1790.

[2] For this and subsequent quoted passages see *Life and Writings of Henry Fuseli*, ed. by John Knowles, 3 vols., 1831.

is certainly no critic". Having said all this, and more, he delivered a lecture on Ancient Art which occupies nearly fifty octavo pages, the greater part of which consists of elaborate analyses of recorded paintings, based largely (like biographies of Shakespeare) on hypotheses —"such, no doubt," he says, "was the 'Paris' of Euphranor . . . the acute inspector, the elegant umpire of female form, receiving the contested pledge with a dignified pause or with enamoured eagerness presenting it to the arbitress of his destiny, was probably the predominant idea of the figure"; like Sir Sidney Lee when dealing with the facts of Shakespeare's life, he presents the reader with all the traditions and allows him to make his choice. And he, like everyone else of his contemporaries, ends up with the Laocoön . . . "every beauty of virility . . ."

The Laocoön, both the sculpture and Winckelmann's treatise, was a persistent influence; nearly forty years earlier, in 1765, Fuseli had published a translation of Winckelmann. Yet Fuseli's academic activities were not confined to antiquity, for in his lecture on the Art of the Moderns, he dealt with Italian, French, German and English critics in a manner calculated to disturb all the more orthodox of the students. Vasari, for example, was "loquacious, lacking in discrimination, over-generous with superlatives, inaccurate in memory and niggardly with information"; Du Fresnoy "spent his life in composing and revising general aphorisms in Latin classical verse" and from his text, affirmed Fuseli, "none ever rose practically wiser than when he sat down to study"; while De Piles merely displays what can be learnt from precept and rule, for the benefit of timorous but academic students.

Of German critics he said "about the middle of last century (*i.e.* the 18th) [they] began to claim the exclusive privilege of teaching the art"; and that "the verdicts of Mengs and Winckelmann became the oracles of Antiquaries, Dilettanti and Artists". Winckelmann himself he described as the "parasite of Mengs", and Mengs as being "better fitted to comment a classic than to give lessons in art". And of English critics he affirmed that "the last is undoubtedly the first"; the volumes of Reynolds "can never be consulted without profit". It was Reynolds who had given him, fresh from divinity experiments in Berlin with Lavater, his first encouragement in the arts. Translator and then accuser of Winckelmann, admirer always of the sculpture called Laocoön yet depreciating authoritatively Winckelmann's famous treatise of the same name, friend and inspirer of Blake, illustrator of Homer, Shakespeare and Milton and painter of the "Nightmare", he produces a complete *Kunstgeschichte* of barely one hundred pages in which he does his best to demolish all the long-accepted standards, and is responsible for nearly a thousand drawings and paintings in most of which he attempts to express his strange, bizarre, romantic vision in Flaxman-classic forms; and he is nearly as successful in that as is Blake.

The tide of Romantic emotion was rising, though not rapidly, but there still persisted the Augustan habit of laying down Rules and searching for Principles; Ideal Beauty was still being pursued. At the end of the eighteenth century, for example, Archibald Alison produced his *Essays on the Nature and Principles of Taste*,[1] which explores the emotions of Sublimity and Beauty

---

[1] Published in Edinburgh, 1790.

as exemplified by sounds, colours, forms, motions, gesture, grace and the human countenance and figure; after four hundred and twenty-three pages of exploration he concludes that artists have to "exalt their conceptions to the imagination of forms more pure and more perfect than any that Nature herself ever presents to them. It is in this pursuit that Real Beauty is at last perceived, which it is the loftiest ambition of the artist to feel and to express." He then emphasises the importance of blending the "emotions of taste" with "Moral sentiment", so that "one of the greatest pleasures of which we are susceptible is made finally subservient to moral improvement". In his insistence on an improvement upon Nature he spoke as Hogarth or Jonathan Richardson might have spoken; but to bring in "moral improvement" was to go further even than Reynolds ever went, with all his insistence on the lofty and the elevated; it was anticipating all the most confused thinking of the nineteenth century, that stage when morals, considered purely as morals, were confounded with art as an expression of something in the artist's mind. And it must be admitted that Alison added little to the argument on either side by his final conclusion that "the Beauty and Sublimity which is felt in the various appearances of matter are finally to be ascribed to their being, either directly or indirectly, the signs of those qualities of mind which are fitted to affect us with pleasing or interesting emotion".

Richard Payne Knight also, and inevitably, produced an *Analytical Enquiry into the Principles of Taste*.[1] He analyses the pleasures and pain of the different Senses, he examines the association of such Ideas as perception,

[1] 1808.

imagination, judgment, the Passions produced by the sublime, the pathetic, the novel, the ridiculous, he investigates the causes of Beauty, not in "the strict and narrow sense in which Burke uses the word, but in the widely used general sense", and at the end of it all he is forced, reluctantly, to the conclusion that Ideal Beauty does not exist, differentiating himself thereby from the majority of his contemporaries and nearly all his predecessors. Payne Knight does, nevertheless, maintain that "there are certain standards of excellence which every generation subsequent to their first production has uniformly recognised in theory . . . such are the precious remains of Greek sculpture, which afford standards of real beauty, grace and elegance, in the human form". And immediately he proceeds to demolish his own argument by saying, with considerable truth, "the sable Africans view with pity and contempt the marked deformity of the Europeans". He can ridicule too, those who would improve on Nature's own work, for "at one time", he remarks, "man crops the tail and ears of his horses and dogs, and at another forces them to grow in forms and directions which nature never intended; his trees and shrubs are planted in fantastic lines, or shorn into the shapes of animals or implements; and all for the sake of beauty. Happily for the poor animals it has never appeared possible to shear them into the shapes of plants, or it would without doubt have been attempted; and we should have been as much delighted at seeing a stag terminating in a yew-tree as ever we were at seeing a yew-tree terminating in a stag."

Knight, however, was at heart more of a "naturalist" than a theoriser, and probably his final views are to be found in his comment on Addison's observation, "though there are several wild scenes that are more delightful than any artificial shows, yet we find the works of Nature still more pleasant the more they resemble Art".[1] That is the true Augustan view, yet as Knight says, to admit that any wild scene could be more delightful than any artificial is bold scepticism for so cautious a writer in that age. Knight then adds a footnote, in which he said "his [Addison's] natural feelings soon rose up against his acquired opinions; and towards the close of the same paper he adds 'I do not know whether I am singular in my opinion; but for my own part I would rather look upon a tree in all its luxuriancy and diffusion of boughs and branches than when it is thus cut and trimmed into a mathematical figure; and cannot but fancy that an orchard in flower looks infinitely more delightful than all the little labyrinths of the most finished parterre'". Addison may have found but few authoritative supporters in taking up that rather revolutionary attitude, but Knight, nearly a century later, would have found many to agree with him; it is, however, equally certain that he would, even so late, have found many to disagree.

[1] *Spectator*, No. 414.

CHAPTER IX

REGENCY

WHEN the disciples of Winckelmann, "Athenian" Stuart
and Sir William Hamilton tried to turn away the rulers
of Taste from the Romans and the Etruscans towards
the Greeks, they were much helped by the politico-
philosophical views prevailing over the greater part of
Europe. Monarchy, as a form of government, was being
very critically examined and the criticism was not, on
the whole, favourable; the newly established republic
in North America was working well enough to call
forth from many quarters an envious admiration;
George III had failed to justify his interpretation of
sovereignty, Louis XVI was being held responsible for
the abuses of his predecessors, the thrones of Spain and
the Sicilies were being rudely shaken by discontented
subjects, and even the ruler of the Papal territories
had to support his prestige more by his spiritual than
his temporal authority; only in some of the German
Grand Duchies was there satisfaction with the traditional order. It was natural, in the circumstances,
that the Greek city-states should seem to provide a
solution, for, remote in time, their mistakes might
well seem insignificant when compared with their
glorious achievements; and that the most conspicuous
of these achievements were in the arts and in letters,
in philosophy and the sciences, demonstrably argued that
their political system produced a high degree of civilisa-

tion; every critic, anyone who had ever attempted an aesthetic philosophy, placed the art of Antiquity above the art of all succeeding ages; therefore, to the academic revolutionary mind, the first condition necessary to the repetition of those achievements was a return to a system of government as like that of the so-called democratic Athens as modern conditions and a larger world would allow.

This new theory of a democracy, in fact, and also others allied to it, were taken up at different times by people who never considered whence such theories had come or what might be their practical application, as by Marie Antoinette and her ladies playing at dairy-farming in their Trianon, translating Rousseau into terms of fashion; the habit of taking such short cuts from a theory to its practice is produced by the same method of thinking as that which, seeing a certain type of building or picture produced by any given political system or religious belief, concludes that the ideas behind that system or belief can only be conveyed by that one type of architecture or of painting, and by no other. Pugin and Ruskin, seeing the abbeys and cathedrals built in an age of unquestioning faith, concluded that the only type of building for a Christian people was the Gothic; a hundred years earlier the Augustans, lacking guidance and looking instinctively to Rome as the inheritor of a tradition, held Raphael or Michelangelo to be the only guides; the makers of the French Revolution found their political ideal in Greece, and Grecian art was henceforth the best expression of all who upheld the Revolution; but just as the Grecian was not infrequently confused with the Roman, so the politics of Athens or Corinth or Sparta were merged, in Paris, into those of Rome; the republic became a consulate, and the consulate an empire.

David, occupying the position of official painter to the Revolution, continued as official painter to the Emperor; henceforward so long as the Empire lasted, and even for some years afterwards, the arts of Greece and Rome were the model for France and therefore for the rest of the civilised world; the Directory, the campaign in Egypt with the consequent outbreak of sphinxes and obelisks and general minor Egyptology, the Consulate and then the Empire, all were witnesses to the marriage between politics and art; circumstances were, as it happened, particularly favourable, since for some years before the Revolution there were, as we have seen, signs of a returning classicism, at any rate in the decorative arts. In France what had been merely a tendency was turned by political events into the almost universally accepted order. In England there were no such violent political changes; but despite our insularity, despite our very general hatred and dread of the Revolution, despite even war, we still looked to France for guidance in taste and fashion as we had done since 1660. For ten years after 1793 personal contact with France was impossible, but the Peace of Amiens in 1803 enabled Englishmen once more, for a few months, to travel over the Continent, to Paris, Florence or Rome; war broke out again in 1804 and lasted for eleven more years, but those few months were enough for the French fashions to cross the Channel. It must also be remembered that there was not, during the Napoleonic wars, a feeling of hostility towards everything French as there was in the war of 1914–18 towards everything German; the novels of

Jane Austen and the majority of the letters of the period hardly suggest the acute consciousness of being at war with which we ourselves were so familiar. Not only was there an absence of hostility towards things French but the traditional superiority of France in matters of taste was not in the smallest degree impaired by the war; and in addition, the war gave new encouragement to the game of collecting in this country.

As the French armies advanced through Piedmont or across the Alps into Lombardy and the Papal territories, or as the British armies advanced from Portugal into Spain and on towards the Pyrenees, they were followed by other armies, the armies of the collectors' agents and dealers in works of art; dwellers in the invaded areas, panic-stricken, were anxious to turn their goods into some more portable form of wealth, while at the same time victorious generals usually celebrated their victories by looting the palaces of the vanquished, and of course it was always possible that the victors might in turn be defeated, and their booty again be looted, or at the worst purchased very cheaply. Although these acquisitive camp - followers undoubtedly faced many real dangers the prizes made any risk worth while, and shiploads of treasures found their way to England, for, though there was some risk of capture at sea, the English fleets were a very fair guarantee of safety. And since England was one of the few countries not invaded by the French; and since, therefore, there was no sudden dispersal of English capital; and since, thanks to the Industrial Revolution and despite our subsidising of most of our allies, there was a considerable amount of money in this country, England became the natural and obvious goal for most of what had been so advantageously secured by the campaigning dealers. Many men, whose fathers had been poor, benefited by the war to the extent of becoming millionaires; and, like new millionaires in all ages and in all countries, they invested very largely in works of art. A new wave of collecting spread over the country; new houses were built to accommodate the new collections, and the houses were, of course, furnished in the taste that fashion demanded. And it happened in addition that we had at this fortunate moment, what has been rare in this country, a Prince who could stamp his name and his personality on his age; with the result that what in France was identified with the taste of those who made the Emperor's taste was translated into English, modified in accordance with our tradition, and renamed after the Regent.

George and his great architect Nash, dictators of the new taste, began by remodelling much of the western part of London; town-planning was easy when carried out by an architect to whom alone it had been entrusted by a Prince who possessed vision and could assume authority; it must be admitted that the then newly popular stucco and cast-iron are among the most dangerous instruments a builder can possess, but there was still a tradition of good manners, an instinct of style, to guide and moderate the use of such easy substitutes. Nash and his master left certainly a stucco-covered London, more severe than most Londoners then cared for, a straight-fronted, Ionic, gas-lighted London; but it is the last of London's many transformations that has been able to command respect. All over England spread their influence; newly fashionable bathing resorts on the south coast, inland spas like Cheltenham and Clifton, were dressed in new clothes of stucco, with bow-windows to catch the sun, or verandahs whose roofs might keep it off, forming the only incidents on their pale, severe fronts; this severity and simplicity formed an admirable background for the details of iron balconies or the delicate tracery of the fanlights over the entrance-doors. The flat-pitched roofs, the wide eaves, the Ionic columns, the balconies and the outside shutters, appeared all over outer London, in Camberwell and Clapham and Streatham, in Blackheath and St. John's Wood, in Kensington and Hampstead; they spread through Greenwich into Kent, through Richmond into Surrey, westwards through Marlow and northwards through St. Albans. The more remote country districts were naturally slower to accept the stucco and plaster, but even those with strong local traditions, such as Kent or Hampshire, Devonshire or Gloucestershire, at least adapted, if they did not wholly adopt, the new fashions; certainly by 1820 there was more stucco in England than its populariser Liardet had ever dreamt of. The tendency throughout the latter part of the eighteenth century for urban influences to spread into the country was now intensified into the total submission to suburban influences, the influence, really, of the villa; in the central parts of London itself there was no great change except where the very character of a district was transformed by demolition or rebuilding, as in what became Regent Street; or where a tract, till then desolate, was developed for the first time, as was the case when Disraeli's almost forgotten uncle, George Basevi, built much of what is called Belgravia. The streets and houses built by

Nash and Decimus Burton or in the fashion set by their example are, in general, so reticent, so austere, so lacking in the spectacular that they are generally overlooked until they are about to be demolished.

The direct personal influence of the Regent, however, did not as a rule tend towards austerity or reticence; those are not the predominant qualities of, for examples, the Pavilion or Carlton House or of Windsor Castle as he left it. Three architects are responsible for these three palaces: Nash, the pupil of Sir Robert Taylor; Holland, the pupil of Sir John Soane; and Wyatville, the nephew of James Wyatt. Each would possibly have achieved fame in any case—Holland by reason of his work for Samuel Whitbread at Southill, and Wyatville for his additions to Sidney Sussex in Cambridge; but, in fact, the lustre that surrounds them is due to the Prince, whose taste and courage gave them opportunities that occur only to the most favoured, for they were beyond doubt fortunate in their patron. Both severally and together they typify the taste of the Regency, the continued combination of Classic with Gothic, the former being momentarily in the ascendant.

Carlton House had originally belonged to Lord Burlington, and had been bought for Frederick Prince of Wales, being rebuilt by Flitcroft while the grounds were laid out by Kent.[1] After the death of the Princess Dowager of Wales in 1772, the place was neglected until it ceased to be habitable. Eleven years later it was made over as a separate establishment for the Prince of Wales, afterwards George IV; Henry Holland was appointed his architect, and after his death in 1806

[1] The best description of Carlton House is given by W. H. Pyne in *Royal Residences*, vol. iii., 1819.

160

Regency

Nash and Wyatville continued to make alterations. Behind the dignified but unpretentious façade Holland brought together Greece and Rome, Hindostan and China, antique simplicity in an entrance-hall, flamboyant Gothic in a dining-room; sometimes his furniture had the austere grace of a design by Flaxman, sometimes it rivalled Percier and Fontaine.[1] A hall with walls of green and verd-antique, and Ionic columns of brown Siena marble led into anterooms and drawing-rooms of crimson, gold, blue and rose with flowered carpets and hangings of velvet and satin elaborately draped; the sombre richness of the blue-velvet closet, in bronze and blue and gold, contrasted with the magnificent opulence of the crimson drawing-room, in green and crimson, rose and gilded plaster, with buhl and ormolu in every corner; all this, however, might have been achieved by anyone familiar with what was being done in Paris; Holland and his patron showed the inspired confusion of their English taste in the conservatory and the Gothic dining-room. In the latter, slender Gothic columns, with capitals composed of the Prince's plumes, rose to a flat ceiling and thence branched out into richly crocketed and indented brackets from which hung chandeliers throwing their light down on to table and chairs in the Grecian taste. The conservatory, which gave, perhaps, but little opportunity for the cultivation of plants, was built in the manner of a cathedral, in florid, van-vaulted Gothic, with a nave and two aisles; the pillars again had capitals composed of the plumes, and the tracery of the roof

---

[1] *The Designs of Percier and Fontaine*, published in Paris in 1800, are an admirable guide to the more opulent "millionaire" taste of the Directoire period in France and the Regency in England.

was filled in with clear glass; the windows of the north and south sides were of armorial stained glass, the west end was filled with tabernacles, niches and statues, behind each pillar was a tall Gothic candelabrum, and the general effect is described by Pyne as "novel and appropriate". In addition, there was an armoury filled with rare accoutrements and romantic curiosities like the saddle of Hettman Platoff or the dagger of Gengis Khan. And this great house, which might have been a monument to the genius of George IV, was demolished in 1826, six years after its completion; but London had come to hate the King, and the King had forgotten London.[1]

He was happier at Brighton, where Nash had turned for him a villa into the Pavilion.[2] The selection of Brighton probably originated with the Prince's enlightened cook, Louis Weltje; his long service with the Prince sufficiently establishes his excellence as a cook; his perception in other directions is demonstrated by his master sending him to attend sales in Paris and buying most of that furniture for Windsor which is now the envy and despair of French collectors. In 1784 he rented a villa in Brighton and wisely employed Holland to enlarge it; he then bought it outright and in 1788 leased it to his master the Prince, who remained his tenant for nineteen years; after Weltje's death in 1807 George purchased the freehold from the widow and

[1] For Holland's surviving masterpiece, however, see *Country Life*, lxviii. 42, 80, 108; a description of Southill, built for Samuel Whitbread, 1795–1800.

[2] Humphrey Repton, *Designs for the Pavilion at Brighton*, 1808; John Nash, *The Royal Pavilion at Brighton*, 1824 (later these plates were purchased by J. B. Nichols and re-issued for him by E. E. Brayley in 1838); H. D. Roberts, *The Story of the Royal Pavilion*, 1915 (based on the above).

began the transformation that turned the Pavilion into what it now remains. The original villa, as enlarged by Holland, consisted of a central rotunda, with a cupola supported on Ionic columns, and two wings each having two semicircular bays running up from the ground to the eaves; it was, in fact, what would now be described as typical of the Regency. In 1803 the stables[1] were erected by William Porden, in the Hindoo style, and about 1806 the Prince commanded Humphrey Repton to prepare designs and plans for a new Pavilion, but, though these were issued two years later, there was not sufficient money both for buying up the adjacent properties and carrying out the plans; at last, in 1817, Repton's visions were materialised by John Nash, who has posthumously stolen the credit, and the work, superintended by the Prince himself, was practically completed three years later; in 1821 the full, dazzling splendour was seen with the prodigious accompaniment of the new gas-lighting.

Repton, at the time of the Prince's commission, was already in revolt against the severe limitations of the modern style, which, he says,[2] "consists of a plain building with rows of square windows at equal distances; and if to these be added a Grecian cornice, it is called a Grecian building: if instead of the cornice certain notches are cut in the top of the wall, it is called a Gothic building. Thus has the rage for simplicity, the dread of mixing dates and the difficulty of adding ornament to utility alike corrupted and exploded both the Grecian and the Gothic style in our modern buildings."

[1] Now known as the Dome.
[2] Humphrey Repton, *Prefatory Observations to Designs for the Pavilion*, 1808.

Yet five years earlier there had been no revolt in Repton's mind, but only a slight indignation against the intrusion of novelties into the accepted order, for in his *Landscape Gardening* he had divided buildings into the two classifications of Horizontal, which meant the Grecian, and Perpendicular, which meant the Gothic, and had then added "there is indeed a third kind, in which neither the horizontal nor perpendicular lines prevail but which consists of a confused mixture of both: this is called *Chinese*". But five years had effected a change in Repton's standards, never very consistent, bringing to him as to many others dissatisfaction with what had once been the foundations of his artistic beliefs, and destroying his faith in both Grecian and Gothic alike; while he was still uncertain how to replace these exploded styles, he was consulted by Sir Charles Cockerell, the owner of Sezincote in Gloucestershire, who had just returned from India and was anxious to introduce the gardening and architecture he had seen there. Repton, who confessed that the subject was then entirely new to him, studied very carefully the sketches and drawings made actually in India by his friend Thomas Daniell, and decided forthwith that Sezincote should be built in the Hindoo manner. His reasons for this decision, and the effect made on him by Daniell's drawings, are confused and, in the light of his subsequent designs for the Pavilion, not very convincing, but such as they are they can be best expressed in his actual words: "I was pleased at having discovered new sources of beauty and variety, which might gratify that thirst for novelty so dangerous to good taste in any system long established, because it is much safer to depart entirely from any given style, than to adjust changes and modifications in its proportions that tend to destroy its character"; [1] then, after a few remarks about the prevalent rage for Gothic and "the sudden erection of spruce [2] Gothic Villas", he rather surprisingly concludes: "it is not therefore with a view to supersede the known styles that I am become an advocate for a new one, but to preserve their long-established proportions pure and unmixed by fanciful innovations". This does not seem a very exact description of the Pavilion's place in English architecture, but Repton's elaborate defence of the Hindoo as the most suitable style for that particular spot is an interesting example of the instinct in most architects of that confused period to relate their cherished novelties to some respectable and long-established tradition; all Repton's schemes for rebuilding of houses or improvement of parks are prefaced by similar apologies, filled with references to the past, and at Sezincote, where he first realised the possibilities of the Hindoo, he is careful to disclaim responsibility. "Although", he says, "I gave my opinion concerning the adoption of this new style and even assisted in selecting some of the forms from Mr T. Daniell's collection, yet the architectural department at Sesincot of course devolved to the brother [3] of the proprietor, who has displayed as much correctness as could be expected in a first attempt of a new style . . ."; an ingenious defence, which leaves us in doubt whether to give

---

[1] *Prefatory Observations, etc.,* 1808.

[2] This derogatory use of "spruce" occurs previously in Repton's proposals for improvements at Bayham Abbey in 1799: "everyone who has had the misfortune to observe the symmetrical houses at Islington and Clapham will allow that symmetry on a small scale is apt to appear spruce".

[3] Samuel Pepys Cockerell, 1754–1827.

credit to Cockerell or Repton and which, in the event of hostile criticism, shifts the blame back to Daniell.

Thomas Daniell had been employed[1] by a Major John Osborne to design a temple at Melchet Park, dedicated to Warren Hastings, a bust of whom was placed inside.[2] To quote the *European Magazine* for December 1802: "The original design, after the chastest models of Hindoo Architecture, comes, we understand, particularly from Thomas Daniell, Esq. R.A.;[3] it was executed in artificial stone by Mr Rossi". Warren Hastings himself composed the following verses on the occasion:

> Thus, Osborne, though the judgment pause to scan
> The sculptor's skill, but more the Temple's plan,
> Whose chaste simplicity the taste displays
> Of India's sons in India's happier days,
> The permanent impression rests with thee;
> Thine all the praise—Be this enough for me:
>> To bear contented my accomplished lot,
>> Impeached, reviled, acquitted and forgot.

Immediately after he had been inspired by Thomas Daniell thus to advise upon Sezincote, Repton received the Prince's command to visit Brighton; with his head still full of Sezincote, he could not fail to follow the lead given by the already completed Dome, particularly as the Prince had recently received presents of some pieces of Chinese wall-paper which were occasioning a gradual increase of *chinoiserie* behind Holland's classic exterior. It was therefore clear to Repton that the new Pavilion must have an Oriental

[1] The author is indebted for this information to the article by Sir Evan Cotton on the Hindoo Temple at Melchet, in *Bengal: Past and Present*, XI, ii., 1930.

[2] The Temple was removed in 1850; two engravings were made by William Daniell of the Temple itself and the bust within it.

[3] Information about the Daniells is given by Sir William Foster in vol. xix. of the Walpole Society (1931).

character; "although", he says, "the outline of the Dome resembles rather a Turkish mosque than the buildings of Hindostan, yet its general character is distinct from either Grecian or Gothic and must both please and surprise every one not bigoted to the forms of either". The trouble, of course, was that most people were more or less bigoted to the forms of one or the other, and the failure of Sir William Chambers forty years earlier to popularise the Oriental modes, at any rate in architecture, was not an encouragement.

Repton, however, was not discouraged. "When", he explains, "I was commanded to deliver my opinion concerning the style of architecture best adapted for the Pavilion, I could not hesitate in agreeing that neither the Grecian nor the Gothic style could be made to assimilate with what had so much the character of an Eastern building. . . . The Turkish was objectional as being a corruption of the Grecian; the Moorish, as a bad model of the Gothic; the Egyptian as too cumbrous for the character of a villa, the Chinese as too light and trifling for the outside, however it might be applied to the interior. Thus, if any known style were to be adopted no alternative remained but to combine from the Architecture of Hindostan such forms as might be rendered applicable to the purpose." It appears that Repton and the Prince intended to add to what was actually designed and subsequently carried out an Orangery, an Aviary, a Pheasantry and a Chinese Garden facing the sea, but it also appears that the uncertainty from which the architect was suffering at the time of the Sezincote commission had not been dispelled even by the Prince's enthusiasm, for, while he is at such pains to discriminate between the Turkish, the Moorish, the Egyptian, the Chinese and the Hindoo, he later defines Indian Architecture as including "Hindustan, Gentoo, Chinese or Turkish; which latter is a mixture of the other three". Despite the enthusiasm of the Prince and the conscientiousness of his architects, the Pavilion was not very generally admired; Farington,[1] writing in 1818, says "we arrived at Brighton. . . . I walked to the front of the Regent's Palace and found the front nearly in scaffolding. The alterations carrying on were said to be in imitation of the Kremlin at Moscow. If so, that celebrated building must very much resemble some of the Palaces represented in Daniell's *Oriental Scenery*. Whatever this building may appear, its singularity is ill-suited to its situation. Instead of having accompaniments suited to its character, every building contiguous to it is of a common ordinary English form and appearance."

The labels of architects matter, after all, but little; Hindoo or Grecian, the Pavilion and Carlton House epitomise the Regency in the person of the Regent himself; in these he, and those he inspired, created something personal and new. At Windsor, on the other hand, they faced with equal success another problem, that of adapting to changed conditions and without violent transformation something traditional and almost sacred. By the end of the reign of George III the Castle, regarded as either a private or a State residence, was almost impossible;[2] yet its existence was nearly synonymous with that of the throne itself. Founded by the first undisputed King of England, occupied by each of

[1] *Diary*, viii. 197.
[2] For this and all architectural information about Windsor see W. H. St. John Hope, *Architectural History of Windsor Castle*, 1913.

his successors, its thirty-fourth successive tenant decided, immediately upon his accession, to make of this incommodious fortress a palace worthy of the first Sovereign in Europe. This princely design was thrown open to competition, a Royal Commission was appointed, and in the course of 1824 the plans of Jeffrey Wyatt were chosen; the same day Wyatt was magnified into Wyatville and was granted an augmentation of arms. His original estimate was about £122,000; by 1830 the bill amounted to £622,000. This additional burden of about £100,000 a year added considerably to the already great difficulties of the Prime Minister, Lord Liverpool, and his immediate successors, but it did result in giving England what is probably the major inhabited royal residence in Europe. The acute military mind of the Conqueror had selected, for strategic reasons, the site; the Plantagenets had built and fortified; the Tudors and the Stuarts civilised; the first three Hanoverians neglected, and the Castle fell nearly into decay. Then Norman, mediaeval and Renaissance were remodelled by the hands of a nineteenth-century genius, though the destruction of much of Wren's work was a heavy price to pay.

Clearly first among many external improvements was the transformation of the Round Tower; within, the greatest was the Waterloo Chamber, built to accommodate the portraits of the allied sovereigns. It is universally agreed that, from whatever viewpoint, the Round Tower gives the Castle its necessary emphasis, that it is the accent marking the rhythm of the design. "By far[1] the most striking and important of the altera-

---

[1] *Illustrations of Windsor Castle by the late Sir Jeffrey Wyatville*, ed. by Henry Ashton, 1840. Also quoted by St. John Hope.

tions to the exterior of the Castle is raising this noble Tower 33 feet, and crowning it with a machicolated battlement; before the alterations it looked squat and mean, now it takes its place as the characteristic feature of this Royal pile . . . it is worthy of remark, as a proof of the importance of this alteration, as well as the judgment which prompted it, that with scarcely one exception is there any representation of Windsor Castle from Norden[1] and Hollar down to 1830, whether on canvas or paper, in which this Tower is not made to appear a great deal higher than it really was, and of such importance was this feature felt to be by painters and draughtsmen that they all in some measure anticipated in their works the change which has since been made; a change by no means arising out of the other alterations, as the Towers and the general mass of the building remain nearly of the same height as formerly." This improvement was improved upon by the lowering of the ground in the ascent towards the Upper Ward. So Windsor stands, a monument to George IV, erected by himself.

Yet the flavour of an age is to be appreciated as fully from its anonymous or forgotten figures as from its distinguished or illustrious; the Middle Ages live for us through the unnamed builders of the cathedrals, the feudal castles and the tithe-barns at least as vividly as through the lines of Chaucer; the age of Elizabeth cannot be realised only by Spenser and the dramatists, nor by Burleigh and Drake, for if we would recapture its flavour we must read its trivial, ephemeral songs and pamphlets; not study only the palaces like Audley

---

[1] John Norden (1548–1625 ?), *A Description of the Honor of Winsor, etc.,* 1607.

End or Knole, but remember also the farmhouses and the cottages; if we praise the eighteenth century for its taste, we base that praise, not only on specified pictures or great houses or other well-documented and much-written-about productions, but on recollections of some portrait, perhaps, by an artist who may be no more than a name even to the student of obscurities, or on some street-frontage in a market town or a red-brick vicarage seen from the railway.

George IV's regency and reign are as rich in great men as were the epochs of his predecessors; although there was no Chatham, there was a Wellington; there was no Reynolds, no Gainsborough, no Wilson and no Adam, but there were Turner and Constable, Soane and Nash; there were Keats and Shelley, Byron, Wordsworth and Scott; there were Rowlandson and Lawrence, both better artists than generally they would allow themselves to be, and there was Jane Austen; all these are secure in their immortality. To think of the 1820's in terms of its obviously great men only will ensure a picture, but an incomplete and over-dramatised one; Nash, for example, was a great architect, but he was also an office, almost a firm, depending for full expression on a measure of collaboration; sometimes the collaborators were great men, a Chantrey or a Westmacott, sometimes they were men of almost unillumined obscurity, like Bubb.[1] The Guildhall contains a large marble monument to Pitt by this artist, but the Tate Gallery contains the remnants of his frieze for Nash's Opera House in the Haymarket, burnt down in 1867;

---

[1] J. George Bubb. What "J" stands for is not known, nor is anything else about him. His bibliography is limited to an article by Mrs Esdaile in *Artwork*, No. 17 (1929).

made of the inevitable Coade's artificial stone, in high relief, these dancing figures are as truly of the Regency as Byron himself; though in the best neo-classic taste, they are so far from Athens that rather they resemble elegant young ensigns on leave from the Peninsula, dancing in fancy dress with Jane Austen's Miss Bennetts; they are not wholly absurd, they are something more than amusements; they are memorials of the last age in England whose character is stamped courageously and proudly on everything it produced.

Bubb's obscurity is not likely, on the slender grounds of the Haymarket frieze and the Guildhall monument, to be changed for lasting fame; doubtless, in the future, as in the present and the recent past, Regency sculpture will be epitomised in terms of Flaxman, architecture in terms of Nash; but it will be an injustice if Nash's deserved fame obscures the benefits conferred on London by other builders nearly as skilful and quite as scholarly as he; by Decimus Burton, for example, or by George Basevi, whose terraces and crescents in the immediate neighbourhood of Belgrave Square show, with the Regent Park terraces of Nash, Regency London at its best. But when Regency London was modern London and Regent's Park was the newest amenity, it was the Colosseum[1] rather than Chester Terrace that took the eye. Not only was this place of entertainment the most successful of all Decimus Burton's Grecian achievements, not only was it accounted a wonder that a young man of twenty-three should have the power to carry out so ambitious a design, but it possessed a dome a little larger than that of St. Paul's; those, there-

[1] *A Brief Account of the Colosseum in the Regent's Park* was published by the proprietors in 1829.

fore, whose pleasure is to marvel at statistics and dimensions, found in the Colosseum plentiful entertainment; this dome-crowned polygon with its great Doric portico possessed, besides the usual vestibules, saloons, galleries and promenades, a conservatory "calculated to delight the botanist and florist" with all imaginable plants and corals and with fountains and *jets-d'eau*; a marine grotto, or cavern, with roof encrusted with stalactites and walls of rock; an ornamented Swiss cottage, and, the real purpose of the design, a panorama or pictorial history of London, constructed, despite many obvious difficulties, in the dome by Mr E. T. Parris, who, to accomplish this prodigious work, was compelled to "stand in a basket supported by two loose poles, and lifted to a great height by ropes". Unfortunately, though within this splendid Grecian shell was contained enough to please the most exacting romantic, the venture was a failure, and within a few years the Colosseum had ceased to exist. On its site now stands a row of houses in a style at present out of fashion, and therefore generally condemned. The Colosseum has gone, but the Terraces round the Regent's Park introduced, as it might be, by Park Crescent, survive to keep living the memories of a patron and an architect who, working in harmony together, by these alone, had they done nothing else, would have made their age of value to all others.

Yet the circumstances in which they worked were not encouraging; England, brought by the war to the extremes of wealth and poverty simultaneously, was threatened by the dangers of emancipation and reform, haunted still by the ghost of Charles Fox and agitated by Cobbett; the King, blind and mad, was virtually deposed, the political leaders alienated from the throne, the people actively hostile to the Regent and resentful of the rest of the royal family; Byron, the most widely read poet, tirading from his exile against his own country; political opinion divided between a clamorous support of liberalism and a fear-inspired suppression of democracy; half the country shocked by a Prince who could make his consort's morals the subject of a legal inquisition, the other half shocked by a Princess whose morals necessitated such an inquiry. Yet the harm George did in his life reacted mostly on his own family and was repaired, in the course of two generations, by his niece; his political influence, for good or for ill, was negligible, but his influence on our civilisation has made of his regency and reign an epoch of the first importance. With his faculty of alienating most of his friends went that of charming most of his enemies; and for his coarseness of moral perception he compensated with an extraordinary delicacy of artistic perception; unimportant as a statesman, he was supreme as a ruler of taste, and his appreciation, encouragement and patronage were wide enough to include Walter Scott and Jane Austen, the elegant Lawrence and the domestic Wilkie, Nash in Regent Street and Nash in Brighton; in the Grecian or the Gothic his sensibility was equally acute and his authority in Taste sufficient to re-establish for those few years a standard bravely raised against the advancing forces of democracy.

The succeeding reign of William IV and Queen Adelaide coincided with the political and social establishment of the newly enriched industrial middle-class, which, while it produced giants like Peel or Gladstone and was responsible for much of the greatness of England in the nineteenth century, is not distinguished for its ability to discriminate in the Fine or the Applied Arts or in anything covered by the words Taste or Sensibility. But while George IV has a personal share in the artistic distinction of his age, William and Adelaide are not responsible for the lack of distinction that characterises theirs, for George's death gave William a popularity that he had not expected and never previously enjoyed, so novel and at the same time so precarious, that having no wish to risk losing it, he was constrained to play for even greater popularity. In the violent tempest of Reform the old, respected barriers of Taste were pulled down and the well-marked, if divergent, tracks abolished.

CHAPTER X

DEMOCRACY AND THE ARTS

WHEN the Princess Adelaide of Saxe-Meiningen was informed of her betrothal to the Duke of Clarence, she wept;[1] when reminded that her future husband would, in all probability, succeed to the English throne as William IV she could hardly feel that that would bring her happiness; nor, in fact, did it. Her strict upbringing, with its insistence on Sensibility, made it peculiarly difficult to reconcile herself to being always surrounded by her husband's, but not her own, children; hers died, but Mrs Jordan's lived and flourished. The Regent and her other brothers-in-law, though amiable towards her when they chose to be, seemed antipathetic when she compared them with her own family. But, worse than any circumstance in her immediate range of personal experience, was the dark, forbidding background: the temper of the People.

The troubled regency and reign of George IV had been occupied with the problems common to most nations in a post-war period; to apply the analogy of an orchestra, the new conditions caused a change in the *tempo* of the nation's life and, though such a change should not be difficult if the conductor be either skilful or authoritative, it is likely to be disastrous if the conductor be negligent or indeterminate, and George IV, in his last years, was, as a conductor of the political

[1] Mary F. Sandars, *Life and Times of Queen Adelaide*, 1915.

176

orchestra, both negligent and indeterminate; he retired to Windsor or Brighton with Lady Conyngham and, admirable as was the artistic result in both those places, his influence in politics was little more than confusing to the Whigs and irritating to the Tories. His death caused a change of conductors in the midst of a highly intricate and difficult passage, and William IV, though far more conscientious than his brother, was even more uncertain as to the course he should pursue. Moreover, the beginning of his reign in 1830 coincided with the accession to office of the Whig Lord Grey, an ardent advocate of Reform; ardent is perhaps an inappropriate adjective to apply to the cold Northumbrian of sixty-six, but it is certainly applicable to his two chief lieutenants, Lord John Russell in the House of Commons and Lord Durham in the Lords; and although Lord Grey could not by any stretch of imagination be called democratic, he had attacked and routed Wellington in a great speech in favour of Reform, which was the immediate cause of his own translation from Opposition to Government and the ending of a long Tory tradition. The inauguration of King William's reign, therefore, marks the beginning of a new movement in political and social evolution of an importance then unequalled since 1688.

While the English have had a traditional dread of violent revolutionary change, liberty of conscience and the freedom of the individual have always been favourite fetishes with us; we have made our heroes out of the Wyclifs and Jack Cades, the Ridleys and Latimers, Eliots, Pyms and Cromwells; Wilkes went to prison for liberty, Pitt tortured his conscience by repressing it, Byron from the security of a self-imposed exile clamoured for it, Canning gloried in it for other nations;

America had set an example by substituting Washington for George III, which was followed in this critical year of 1830 by France when she substituted Louis-Philippe for Charles X. Liberty, by 1830, had moved out of the romantic stage; it was no longer supported by abstractions about the Rights of Man, but by the enumerations of a set of very definite grievances. Yet it is a mistake to think that these grievances were merely those of an embittered, machine - wrecking mob; certainly the revolution in industrial methods had created such a mob, angry and uncomprehending, largely composed of those who had exchanged the long-familiar poverty of the fields and villages for the bewildering poverty of new slums and factories, but the same revolution, while emphasising the poverty of the very poor, also promoted many to unaccustomed wealth, creating a new and rich middle-class with no traditions but plenty of ambition, who, possessing wealth, not unnaturally demanded power. And power, under a political system unchanged since the Whig Revolution, was denied them; so far as they were concerned, the case for Reform was clear, supported easily enough by the familiar exposure of the illogicalities of rotten boroughs and glaring cases of nepotism, corruption and so forth; and it was not difficult to dismiss the case against it as proceeding either from an hysterical dread of republicanism or from the conservative, traditional habit of obstruction or from the selfish desire of the privileged to keep their possessions to themselves. The word "Democracy" was still used, even by those who later would have been Liberals, as a term of abuse, but it already commanded sufficient respect to imply fear as well as hate.

Democracy and the Arts

This new democratic temper not only made its appearance in social and political life, but it began to invade the arts also. So thorough did the invasion soon become that it might almost be described as the Artistic Revolution; the tyranny of the Greeks and the Romans was thrown aside at last, and inspiration was found in the more popular atmosphere of daily life; the arts, in fact, instead of remaining classical or Renaissance, became modern; *genre* pictures of contemporary subjects began to take the place of the Heroic, the Historic or the Grand; and about 1820 Robert Vernon began to form his famous collection, the first to consist entirely of modern British works; that is to say, it had taken about a hundred years for Hogarth to win a hearing. Yet England was the first country in which this phenomenon, this appearance of a native modern art, occurred; the enthusiasm evoked by Constable's "Haywain" at the Paris Salon of 1824 could only have been evoked from a school still enduring, though with an ill grace, the rules of the *néo-grec* enforced by David and by his followers in Belgium, and it was England, through Constable, who gave the romantic lead for which Delacroix and Géricault had been waiting. A faint, debased classicism still survived in this country both in painting and in the applied arts till at least as late as the Great Exhibition and, in painting, enjoyed a rather unexpected revival in the draped goddesses of Albert Moore and the Roman baths of Alma-Tadema; but, for many years before, these and similar manifestations had belonged to the lanes rather than to the highways of English art-history. Academism, safely on the highways, concerned itself, strangely, with what was in effect a modernist tendency; Turner and Constable, both, though rather reluctantly, accepted by the Academy, set themselves to paint, each in his own manner, what Nature revealed to them rather than what knowledge of other pictures told them; Wilkie recorded scenes from modern rather than ancient times and, when he attempted the historic, portrayed his actors as Scott did his, dressed in the clothes of their time yet as living figures rather than monuments. And the patrons, the collectors and the critics, so far from condemning this new practice, supported it in the most practical way.

The new taste rapidly became as popular as might have been expected; it is obvious that this should have been so, since the painters were making their appeal through those experiences which are common to everyone instead of through those which can only be shared by the learned, the much-travelled or at least the educated; they had abandoned their attempt to edify or improve mankind by means of the Noble or the Tragic and had changed from the Heroic to the Humble, from the Grand to the Domestic. Hogarth, almost a century earlier, had preferred what Reynolds called the Low to what good taste demanded, the Elevated; but he had given his domestic or "low" scenes a monumental quality by the intensity of his moral purpose and the force of his satire. Satire, in a romantic age, was not likely to be popular; even caricature had degenerated from the savage patriotism of Gillray to the generalities of the rather jejune Bunbury. Moral purpose was still there, as it always is in English painting, but the Tragic will always be less popular, in a romantic age, than the Pathetic and in a democratic age it is more generally satisfactory to find the Noble in a humble setting than in the remoter surroundings of antiquity. The England of William IV was as democratic as it was romantic, which is to say that it proceeded to busy itself greatly with the breaking-down of privilege, with the securing of recognition for those who were not privileged and with the closer limiting of those who were; and, with the usual illogicality that never fails to baffle the foreign observer, many of these reformers, as has happened in English history often enough, were themselves of the class they were seeking to enfeeble; others, however, were of the newly enriched commercial and industrial class, so that Whigs and Tories could no longer be distinguished, as they could a hundred years earlier, as the "City" and the "Landed" interests; Reform gave to the parties a new and, in the main, a lasting significance. The French revolutions of 1789 and 1830 were in all men's minds, but to some they pointed the dangers of repressing democracy while to others they showed clearly what would happen if democracy were not suppressed.

Meanwhile the Reform Bill struggled through the two Houses, became at last in 1832 law, and settled into anti-climax. Queen Adelaide's visions of mob-rule and the guillotine were not realised, and the people's visions of liberty and enfranchisement were not realised either. The promoters and supporters of the Bill made it, in fact, clear that their democratic sympathies stopped short at a very early point and that the people had not yet, in their view, reached the stage of development when they could be considered politically to exist; they were, however, promised education. The unfortunate political and social results of that ill-judged gift are not to the point here; what is to the point is that English civilisation was largely in the hands of a new class, thrown up by the eruption of sudden wealth and nourished on the political power given them by Reform. The nineteenth century was to be theirs, as they foresaw, and both the responsibility and the credit must be theirs also.

The Arts, like their new patrons, were beginning to taste a new freedom. After a century and a quarter of control and supervision Taste was set free to go where it would, the old rules were thrown aside and, as yet, no one dreamed of making new ones. There was no lead, not even the transitory guidance of a fashion, for Taste itself went out of fashion; that is to say, adherence to one prevailing taste went out. It is customary to deride fashionable taste, but since there is no permanent canon it follows that all taste is an affair of fashion; whether a given vogue be long- or short-lived is immaterial, for though it may last a decade or a century, or simply be the rage for two seasons, it will vanish in the end. Nothing in Nature and nothing made by man is aesthetically either "good" or "bad" in itself but is only so when it is formally pronounced to be one or the other; certain pictures, poems, views, human beings, wines or buildings are admired by common consent, which necessarily implies a degree of unanimity; but since there can never be absolute unanimity in matters of Taste, what we call common consent is simply the concurrence of the majority with the prevailing fashion. The majority to-day admires Shakespeare or Switzerland or the Taj Mahal, but two centuries ago it was a small minority indeed who found beauty in *King Lear* or the Alps. The majority in any form of opinion is composed principally of people whose minds are inactive and whose senses are blunted, since the majority of human beings on the earth are so constituted; it does not mean that there is an implied lack of intelligence in admiring Raphael or Shakespeare, in being a Hindu in India or a Communist on Clydeside, but it does mean that most people do or are these things for reasons that have no connection with thought but are the result of environment, upbringing or susceptibility to a prevailing atmosphere. Politics and morals can generally be related fairly easily to some universal factor such as, for example, expediency, and the merits or shortcomings of different parties or codes be judged by such a standard; religion, though a common emotion even in the most civilised peoples, has very few such factors, and the Arts, which play a part in the minds of only a small proportion of mankind, have none.

It is probably the realisation of this, that there is no common factor which will make the Arts explicable or acceptable to all men alike, that brought about the invention of Popular Education, which, as we know, consists in imparting stated facts to people more or less eager to acquire such information but generally unable to apply it. Facts can be extracted even from the Arts, and *Kunstgeschichte* can be compressed into a text-book as easily as can the History of Civilisation; with the introduction of photography and other forms of mechanical reproduction, pictures themselves became facts to be learnt as easily as the Kings of England and the plays of Shakespeare, so that everybody could learn about Art without ever having to look at a picture. All men were taught to read, upon compulsion, and very soon the habit of reading was so widespread that it was almost universally indulged in, to the exclusion of other activities such as thinking or seeing, with the result that such of the Arts as are not strictly narrative suffered a decline in prestige. Painting survived, largely because pictures are expensive and their possession implies a certain social standing; the new democratic England patronised its native painters more generously than the old England had done, but it insisted on their producing pictures that were easy to read. Those painters, therefore, who produced the most readily comprehensible narratives, or could satisfy the most widely experienced of the simple emotions, were naturally held in the highest estimation; or rather, perhaps, those painters who could satisfy most simply, and with least effort to the beholder, those feelings that everybody must some time experience.

The expression "simple emotions" is, perhaps, a little meaningless, since every emotion is both simple and complex according to the intensity with which it is felt. It is, however, reasonably clear that those who can and do read but whose response to an experience is not related to any other experience and is not, as a rule, even consciously made, far outnumber either the illiterate or the highly civilised. They, after the industrial revolution, because they were both the largest and the richest section of society, were able to impose their demands on the producers, the creators. The influence of the older Society remained sufficiently strong for the new inheritors of their kingdom to try to ape it in as many respects as possible, to feel, for example, the great importance of possessions; estates, houses, servants, carriages were as easy to acquire for Lancashire industrialists as they had been for East India Company nabobs or South Sea speculators; but while the two latter classes had been able to find a satisfactorily expensive form of display in entering the House of Commons, this, after the passing of Reform, ceased to be *de rigueur* since it no longer implied of necessity either wealth or private interest. Political equality was felt to be a somewhat empty privilege if no social distinction were added to it; but, on the other hand, if politics had lost their prestige, the arts still retained theirs. The "snob-value" of the arts is still one of their most enduring qualities, and was as considerable a century ago as it was earlier or as it is now, but in the age of rigid control those who considered it necessary to be interested in the Arts possessed, as a rule, orderly and active minds accustomed to government, and either inherited or troubled themselves to acquire the sense of proportion which enabled them to dispense with the redundant or the jejune; or if the passion for platitude overcame them, as it often did, they insisted on its being expressed in balanced and well-ordered phrases, valuing the form more highly than the content. Those who had controlled the Rules of Taste were few but, though their taste varied from fashion to fashion, the control had been firm. The rest had either happily ignored or obediently followed.

With this change in the relative "snob-values" of politics and the arts, it was natural that those who, two generations earlier, would have expended their energy and their fortune on attaining social distinction through the House of Commons should now turn their attention to the arts and become patrons and collectors; but since the Connoisseurs and the Persons of Taste no longer exercised their guiding control, and since the new men generally lacked confidence in their own judgment and taste, it was on the whole safer to be a patron rather than a collector, to abandon Old Masters for modern. Not having as yet organised themselves into a controlling body,[1] the dealers were not in a position to assume the authority of the Connoisseurs as it fell from them, and Authority ceased to exist; the collector became a patron the more readily because he could impose his own standards on the artists he was supporting; there were no rules to prove him wrong, no dictators to convict him of lacking taste.

The Reform Bill benefited exclusively and extensively the middle class; while aristocratic existence continued along much the same track as before, with inherited tradition behind it and accumulated experience surrounding it, and while the various degrees of lower class remained unconcerned with anything beyond the immediate needs of the body, it was the middle-class patronage[2] that controlled henceforward for many years the Arts; since the education that these patrons had for the most part received, and which they now promised to their inferiors, did not provide much in the way of visual or intellectual training, the deficiency had to be made up by emphasising in pictures other considerations which previously had been regarded as of secondary importance. First, there was the literary; this indeed had existed in painting since the Renaissance in the sense that every picture that was not simply

[1] The opposition to the purchase of the Elgin Marbles is one of the earliest examples of aesthetic considerations being dominated by commercial; partly it was based on *bona-fide* but mistaken judgment, but partly also on the anxiety of those dealers who had supplied inferior Graeco-Roman pieces as genuine Greek. See Chapter X, *ante*.

[2] Lord Egremont was a patron, but exceptional, since he made Petworth a philanthropic institution as well as a gallery of modern art.

a portrait had a basis of narrative, but the narrative had been hardly more than the foundation on which the artist built his picture; had it been more than that the range of subject-matter would have been far wider than it actually was in the religious, historical or grand painting of the seventeenth and eighteenth centuries. In the new conditions of a democratic society, subject became all-important because the method of presentation or treatment was very generally ignored. Secondly, this literary consideration was itself subject both to the moral and the emotional, which influenced not only painting and sculpture but poetry and the novel as well; the morality was what has come to be called the morality of the middle classes, which is not the self-defensive one of expediency, of the struggle for existence, nor yet that of the philosopher, but the simple codification of the Ten Commandments; in a middle-class society these cease to be a general guide to civilised behaviour, and become the absolute standard by which all conduct is judged. The emotions also were of the same class; not the demonstrative grief or the boisterous and unashamed laughter of the humble, nor the deep feeling and true sense of values of the loftier mind, but the gentility which emasculates tragedy into pathos. It was not, of course, a new phenomenon; but what had been an intermittent tendency of one age became the salient characteristic of the next. It is inevitable that, for economic reasons, whenever active patronage of living artists exists at all, the artists should conform to the standards and demands of their patrons. The number of artists prepared to starve for their own ideals, like Haydon, is smaller than is generally supposed, and if an artist is left to starve it is more often because he is an inferior painter than because he is an unappreciated idealist. This new patronage, therefore, meant that academic art, that is, the form of art produced by the majority of artists and officially approved by the purchasing public, conformed in every respect to the not very exalted standards imposed on them by their market.

There was, as might have been expected, a revolt; but the pre-Raphaelite rebellion was not successful in its ambition of revolutionising a debased official art, and Millais himself in due course became president of an Academy essentially the same as that which had been so profoundly disturbed by his "Carpenter's Shop". Understanding by "Academic" art the nineteenth-century equivalent of what in the eighteenth century had been called the "Correct" taste, it is worth noting that what posterity has held to be the finest and most important works of the English eighteenth century are those in the Correct taste, excepting the work of Hogarth; while what we now consider the finest works of the English nineteenth century are the fruits of revolt, excepting the work of Alfred Stevens. It is clearly unwise to reply on the permanence of our present taste, but, judged by that standard, which is really the only one possible for us, it would seem that the effect on academic painting, and on the taste of a society produced by the conditions of a democratic régime, is less favourable than that produced by an aristocratic and oligarchic régime.

This result, in England, is almost certainly produced by the relaxation of control by the few, by the abandonment of guidance on the part of the many; that may not be the sole cause, but it is demonstrable that public taste in every one of the arts was firmly controlled under the oligarchies of the eighteenth century, and that control from the same sources was abandoned or at least ineffective under the system of democratic government, popular education and a widely extended franchise. But the lowering of the standards both of taste and of production which coincides with the relaxing of control is perhaps in part due to other causes, or rather to a more general cause which may be identified with that widely diffused spirit of romanticism whose relation to democratic doctrine is almost parental. The English temperament, at least since the twelfth century, has included a marked strain of individualism, manifesting itself in a resentment against the dictation of alien or extraneous authority in religion or politics, which has ensured us against violent change and made recourse to revolution only necessary when proposed changes have been reactionary. Even in the arts, where our development has been slow and the general interest and knowledge small, the process has been to absorb foreign influence into the native tradition, and not *vice versa*. When Reform gave an additional impulse to the romantic-democratic spirit, it was not unnatural that the authority of Antiquity should be discarded, but it was not in the nature of the English intellect to provide a substitute nor, indeed, of the new temperament to consider such substitute necessary. Certain painters of outstanding individuality, such as Constable, found opportunities which could never have occurred to them earlier, but it was left to other nations with a stronger intellectual or classical tradition, such as France, to make the highest use of their discoveries; it was those nations that had perhaps suffered most from the tyranny of the Greeks and the Romans that benefited most therefrom.

If individualism be a virtue, it is reasonable to presuppose an individuality; when that is lacking, as in the case of the majority of painters perhaps it is, the alternative to classic authority is no longer romantic enterprise but continued subjection to yet other authority. Reynolds and Richard Wilson, while surrendering to the authority of Antiquity or to the Renaissance interpreters of that authority, conditioned their surrender in the terms of their Englishness, their modernity, their personal vision; Turner achieved his highest (which he reached while George IV was still living) by calling Claude and Poussin to his assistance; when, like Constable, he was impelled only by his vision and forbade his intellect to speak, he became one of those directly responsible for the sterilising of the art, for the belief that the greatest painter is the most faithful, the most meticulous reflector of natural phenomena; responsible, that is to say, in circumstances where constructive criticism is absent. In a society that has lost, or has never possessed, the faculty of thinking, such criticism is not likely to exist, and in a democratised society where the outward signs of education are more generally accessible, thinking, as a conscious process, is not always very widely practised. The careers of Benjamin Robert Haydon and Sir David Wilkie are illuminating in this context: the former ignored the new tendencies, clung to his belief in the Grand, the Noble and the Elevated, painted pictures that were widely praised and seldom sold, believed passionately in his heroics, and in despair destroyed himself; Wilkie surrendered to democratic tastes, poured his genius into the mould chosen for him by his public, and succeeded. Haydon would probably never have been a great painter, but he would have been a better one had he been given his opportunity; he was the victim of fashion because his art was unfashionable, but had he lived in a day when fashions in taste were controlled by a few men instead of by a whole class it is almost certain that he, and through him English art, would have benefited immeasurably. Wilkie, too, was a victim of fashion, in that the collectors of such an epoch as his (and subsequently) leaned markedly towards the seventeenth-century Dutch painters, while insisting that they should be translated into nineteenth-century English terms; set free from those conditions, from the necessity of being trivial, Wilkie might have been a giant among painters.

In his own day Wilkie was great; half a century ago he was of no account; a decade hence he will again be given greatness; he is not of those very few who are now beyond the fluctuations of taste. Taste in its wide sense is an affair of fashion, in its narrow sense an affair of discrimination, and discrimination itself is generally affected by, if not actually based on, the influence of fashion. Judgment of craftsmanship in architecture, in painting, in sculpture, in music or in carpentry, is pronounced in relation to standards that may fairly be called permanent, but in our consideration of the ends to which such craftsmanship may be employed there is no permanence. Certain peoples have had a continuity of civilisation which has underlain all the successive changes of fashion; others, ourselves included, are younger in that respect and have not been able to rest their fashions on so solid or so permanent a basis.

Instinct being absent, acknowledged leadership must take its place, and the qualifications for such leadership are not such as can be readily or easily acquired; it must be authoritative, with an understanding of the source whence its authority is derived. Throughout the period under discussion it was almost an axiom among men of wealth that they must patronise the Arts, but on the distribution of wealth depended the form such patronage was to take; the artist worked, as he will continue to work, for his patron, and he will work down to him as easily as he will work up to him; he sets himself his own standard of execution, but its application will generally be in accordance with contemporary criticism; and the criticism to which the majority of painters, architects or other artists are most sensitive is, as a rule, that of the people for whom they are working, and on whom they are dependent.

BIBLIOGRAPHY

Architecture

ADAM, ROBERT and JAMES. Works. 1773–8 and 1822.

BLOMFIELD, SIR REGINALD. History of Renaissance Architecture in England. 1897.

BOLTON, ARTHUR T. The Architecture of Robert and James Adam. 1922.

CAMPBELL, COLIN. Vitruvius Britannicus. 1725–70.

CHAMBERS, SIR WILLIAM. Treatise of Civil Architecture. 1759.

CLARKE, KENNETH. Gothic Revival. 1928.

DALLAWAY, REV. J. Observations on English Architecture. 1806.

EASTLAKE, CHARLES. History of the Gothic Revival in England. 1872.

HOPE, W. H. ST. JOHN. Architectural History of Windsor Castle. 1913.

KENT, WILLIAM, and BURLINGTON, 3RD EARL OF. Designs of Inigo Jones. 1727.

LANGLEY, BATTY. Treasury of Designs. 1740.

PAINE, JAMES. Plans and Elevations of Noblemen's Houses. 1783.

RAMSEY, S. C. Small Houses of the late Georgian Period. 1924.

RICHARDSON, A. E., and GILL, C. L. Regional Architecture in the West of England. 1924.

RUTTER, JOHN. Delineations of Fonthill. 1823.

SCOTT, GEOFFREY. The Architecture of Humanism. 1914.

SWARBRICK, JOHN. Robert Adam and his Brothers. 1915.

WARE, ISAAC. The Complete Body of Architecture. 1735–60.

Painting and Sculpture

BELL, CLIVE. Landmarks in Nineteenth-Century Painting. 1927.

BRAY, ANNA ELIZA. Life of Thomas Stothard, R.A. 1851.

CHRISTIES, MESSRS. Catalogue of the Sale of the Lansdowne Marbles. 1930.

DALLAWAY, REV. JAMES. Anecdotes of Painting in England. 1826.

ESDAILE, MRS K. A. Monumental Sculpture in England. 1928.

—— Roubiliac. 1929.

HAMILTON, SIR WILLIAM. Collection of Engravings from Ancient Vases. 1791.

HOGARTH, WILLIAM. Analysis of Beauty. 1753.

193

KNOWLES, JOHN. Life and Writings of Henry Fuseli. 1831.
METEYARD, ELIZA. Life of Josiah Wedgwood. 1866.
REYNOLDS, SIR JOSHUA. Discourses. 1797.
RICHARDSON, JONATHAN. Theory of Painting. 1715.
SMITH, J. T. Nollekens and his Times. 1828.
VERTUE, GEORGE. MS. Notebooks. Walpole Society *passim*.
WALPOLE, HON. HORACE. Anecdotes of Painting. Collected Works, vol. iii. 1798.
—— Aedes Walpolianae. 1747.
WHITLEY, W. T. Artists and their Friends in England, 1700–1799. 1928.
—— Art in England, 1800–1820. 1929.

Landscape Gardening

CHAMBERS, SIR WILLIAM. Dissertation on Oriental Gardening. 1772.
KYP, JOHANNES, and KNYFF, LEONARD. Britannia Illustrata, or Noblemens Seats. 1709.
MANWARING, ELIZABETH. Italian Landscape in Eighteenth-Century England. 1925.
REPTON, HUMPHREY. Theory and Practice of Landscape Gardening. 1803.
—— A Letter to Uvedale Price, Esq. 1794.
WALPOLE, HON. HORACE. Observations on Pleasure-Grounds. 1774.
—— Treatise on Modern Gardening. Collected Works, vol. ii. 1798.

Chinoiserie

CHAMBERS, SIR WILLIAM. Designs for Chinese Buildings. 1757.
—— Dissertation on Oriental Gardening. 1772.
CORDIER, HENRI. La Chine en France. 1910.
GUERIN, J. La Chinoiserie en Europe au XVIIIme siecle. 1911.
LENYGON, F. The Chinese Taste in English Decoration. *Art Journal*, 1911.
PILLEMENT, JEAN. Livre de Chinois. 1758.
—— Cahier de barques et chariots chinois. 1770.
PYNE, W. H. History of the Royal Residences. Pubd. 1829.
Union Centrale des Arts Decoratifs (Paris). Le Gout chinois en Europe.

General

ALISON, ARCHIBALD. Nature and Principles of Taste. 1790.
ALLEN, GEORGE. Occasional Thoughts on Genius. 1749.

Bibliography

BURKE, EDMUND. Essay on the Sublime and Beautiful. 1756.

CUST, SIR LIONEL, and COLVIN, SIR SIDNEY. History of the Society of Dilettanti. 1898.

FARINGTON, JOSEPH. Diary. 1793–1821.

GILPIN, WILLIAM. Essays on Picturesque Beauty. 1794.

—— Observations on the Picturesque. 1798.

GREEN, VALENTINE. Review of the Polite Arts in France compared with their Present State in England. 1782.

GWYN, J. Essay on Design. 1749.

HAYDON, B. R. Journal. 1853.

HUSSEY, CHRISTOPHER. The Picturesque. 1927.

JESSEN, PETER. Rococo Engravings. 1922.

JOURDAIN, MISS M. English Decoration and Furniture of the Late Eighteenth Century. 1922.

KNIGHT, RICHARD PAYNE. Analytical Enquiry into the Principles of Taste. 1808.

PRICE, SIR UVEDALE, BART. Essay on the Picturesque. 1794, 1798, 1810.

PYNE, W. H. History of the Royal Residences. Pubd. 1829.

REYNOLDS, SIR JOSHUA. Letters. Ed. F. Whiley Hilles, 1929.

RICHARDSON, JONATHAN. Art of Criticism. 1719.

—— Science of a Connoisseur. 1719.

ROBERTS, H. D. Story of the Royal Pavilion. 1915.

ROUQUET, —. L'État des Arts en Angleterre. 1755.

SANDARS, MARY F. Life and Times of Queen Adelaide. 1915.

SHAFTESBURY, 3RD EARL OF. Letter Concerning Design. 1732.

SUGDEN and EDMONDSON. History of English Wallpaper. 1926.

Walpole Society. Publications. 1912 to date.

INDEX

197

The Rule of Taste

198

Index

Index

The Rule of Taste

Index

THE END